A TASTE OF
PERSIA

A TASTE OF
PERSIA

AN INTRODUCTION TO
PERSIAN COOKING

NAJMIEH K. BATMANGLIJ

MAGE PUBLISHERS

LIBRARY OF CONGRESS CATALOGING-IN-PUBLICATION DATA

Batmanglij, Najmieh.
A taste of Persia: an introduction to Persian cooking
Najmieh K. Batmanglij. — 1st ed.
p. cm.
Includes index.
ISBN 0-934211-54-X
1. Cookery, Iranian.
I. Title
TX725.I7B377   1999
641.5955 — dc21
98-31208
CIP

FIRST EDITION
SECOND PRINTING

Printed and manufactured in Korea

Mage books are available at bookstores or directly from the publisher.
To receive our latest catalogue, call toll free 1-800-962-0922
or visit Mage online at www.mage.com.

TABLE OF CONTENTS

INTRODUCTION

This book is an invitation to the world's other ancient cuisine. Persia's cookery, like China's, has had thousands of years of change and refinement, but it still retains roots in its ancient sources. As a matter of fact, you know more about Persian food than you might think. When you ask for oranges, pistachios, spinach, or saffron, you are using words derived from the Persian that refer to foods either originating in the region or introduced from there, for Persia was a great entrepôt of the ancient and medieval worlds. The land was the first home of many common herbs, from basil to coriander, and to scores of familiar preparations, including sweet and sour sauces, kababs, and almond pastries.

Such preparations are most delicious in their original forms, which you will find in the recipes in this book. All the recipes come from the land Europeans have long called Persia. That name is the Hellenized form of Pars, the southwestern province that was the homeland of the rulers of the first Persian empire. They, however, called themselves Iranians and their country Iran, words derived from Aryan, the name of their ancestral tribes. Nowadays the words are used interchangeably. They describe a people whose civilization and cuisine are ancient indeed.

A FEW THOUSAND YEARS AT A GLANCE

By 1000 BCE, when the Indo-Aryan tribes called the Medes and the Persians first settled the highlands of the Iranian plateau, the region had been home to great civilizations for thousands of years. In Iran itself, kingdoms had risen and fallen. Among them was the mysterious and widespread civilization whose kings were buried in elaborate tombs at Marlik, near the Caspian Sea, in the second millennium BCE. The people of Marlik produced splendid jewelry, armor, and tools; their gold and silver eating and drinking vessels often displayed the animal motif that remained part of the Iranian tradition. And the styles of their everyday kitchen equipment—some of which is shown on these pages—are echoed in the region today.

Designed so efficiently that the same style is still in use 4000 years later, this stone pestle from Marlik has a spout for pouring off such local delicacies as pomegranate juice and olive oil.

We know much more about ancient Elam (present-day Khuzistan, known as "the land of sugar cane"), rich in trade. Elam's famed cities were Susa in the lowlands close to Mesopotamia; and Anshan in the Zagros Mountains, set among vineyards, stands of almond and pistachio, and fields of wheat, barley, and lentils. To the northwest was the fertile flood plain of Mesopotamia, where power surged back and forth between the empires of Babylonia and Assyria.

By 2000 BCE, such utensils as this bronze pot and hanging ladle were in common use at Marlik and other kingdoms in what is now Iran.

Archeology and the cuneiform inscriptions left for posterity tell us much about life in these royal cities. From ninth century BCE Assyrian Nimrud, for instance, come the records of Ashurnasirpal II. In between unnervingly vivid accounts of the lands he had destroyed and the people he had savaged, Ashurnasirpal took care to describe a 10-day feast he had staged at Nimrud. Always grandiose, he claimed it was for "47,074 persons, men and women, who were bid to come from

A seventh century BCE frieze from Nineveh immortalizes the sumptuous pleasures of the Assyrian court. Here Ashurbanipal and his queen, attended by musicians, dine in an arbor among vines, palms, and pomegranates.

across my entire country," plus thousands more foreign and local guests. The menu included thousands of cattle, calves, sheep, lambs, ducks, geese, doves, stags, and gazelles. There were also items familiar today: bread, onions, greens, cheese, nuts, fresh fruits including pomegranates and grapes, pickled and spiced fruits, and oceans of beer and wine.

This king's descendant, Ashurbanipal, would announce his destruction of the Elamite capital 200 years later ("Susa, the great holy city.... I conquered. I entered its palaces, I dwelt there rejoicing; I opened the treasuries.... I destroyed the ziggurat... I devastated the provinces and their lands I sowed with salt."). By then, however, the tide of history was turning, and the ever-warring Mesopotamian kings were soon to meet their Mede and Persian masters.

Conquests began in the seventh and sixth centuries BCE, when the Medes joined Babylon to subdue the Assyrians; the Medes' cousins, the Persians, then overcame

Babylonia and went on to conquer Croesus, the famously rich king of Lydia in today's Turkey. The Persian King Cyrus the Achaemenid and his successors expanded the empire until, by the time of Darius, it was the largest the world had yet known. In 522 BCE, Darius' territory, centered on the Persian heartland of Fars, covered two million square miles from the Black Sea to the Persian Gulf, from the Nile in Egypt to the Indus in India. It was the richest of empires: The Greek historian Herodotus, writing in the fifth century BCE, estimated that annual tribute of slaves, animals, foodstuffs, textiles, spices, metals, and gems amounted to a million pounds of silver. And it was ably governed from such cities as Susa (splendidly rebuilt), Babylon, Ecbatana (modern-day Hamadan), and Persepolis on the Persian plateau. A Pax Persica lay over most of the known world.

Persia also inherited the civilizations of the past; they absorbed and transformed the arts of Mesopotamia and Egypt, Lydia and the Greek colonies of Ionia on the Turkish coast. The Persian empire's rulers were true cosmopolitans, as

Herodotus' contemporary Xenophon noted in describing their cookery. The Persians, he wrote, "have given up none of the cooked dishes invented in former days; on the contrary, they are always devising new ones, and condiments as well." He added, apparently with surprise, that they kept cooks just to invent dishes, along with butlers, confectioners, and cupbearers to serve at table.

For the renown of their cookery, the Persians had Darius and his successors to thank. What we know of Achaemenid cuisine is rather sketchy—we hear of vast banquets at Persepolis where roast camel and ostrich breast were served—but it is clear that the ancient Persians cherished food. Darius paid attention to agriculture. His engineers renewed the irrigation canals that watered his provinces; he expanded the age-old system of underground aqueducts called

A procession of tribute bearers from the far reaches of his vast empire is carved on the staircase of the reception hall of Darius the Great (r. 522-486 BCE) at Persepolis. This man with his mysterious container—perhaps for precious spices—is a Mede.

qanats that brought mountain water to the dry Iranian plateau; and he urged experimentation and the transport of seeds and plants. To feed the famed Persian horses, alfalfa seeds were exported to Greece; indeed, it is said that the Persian empire could expand because its rulers carried with them the alfalfa seeds to sow for their mounts. To feed humans and for pleasure, plants were transported from province to province: Rice was imported from India to Mesopotamia, sesame from Babylon to Egypt, fruit trees from the Zagros Mountains to Anatolia, pistachios from Fars to Syria.

There was also commerce far beyond the borders of empire, for the great trade routes that linked Mesopotamia to China in the east and India in the southeast all met in Persia. This trade continued—it even expanded—through Persia's decline and fall to Alexander in 331 BCE, through the rule of Alexander's Hellenistic successors, the Seleucids, and their successors, the Parthians who came from Khorasan in Eastern Iran. It flourished during the restoration of the Persian empire achieved by the Sasanian dynasty in the third century CE. From India, for instance, came rice and sugar cane, peacocks and the wild jungle fowl that became the domestic chicken. There was a healthy caravan trade with China. Persian horses (and the alfalfa to feed them), and Persian grapevines appeared there in the second century BCE; in the centuries that followed, Parthian and Sasanian traders introduced the walnut, pistachio, pomegranate, cucumber, broad bean and pea (known in China as the "Iranian bean"), as well as basil, coriander, and sesame. Among the plants that came from China in return, to be disseminated westward to Greece, Rome, and Byzantium by the Persians, were peaches, apricots, tea and rhubarb.

The Sasanians of the sixth and seventh century dined in splendid style, with the silver spoons and forks (which later went out of fashion) shown here. The handle ends are ornamented with animal heads, an ancient Iranian motif.

Such delicious importations marked the luxurious civilization of the Sasanian era. The dynasty built magnificent palace-cities in its homeland of Fars. Their imperial court, however, was at the palace of Ctesiphon not far from what became Baghdad. It was a byword for splendor. Its marble-floored throne room was covered by a 110-foot-high vault, the tallest ever built; the winter carpet was designed in the form of a garden with gems for flowers. The king's throne was set on the backs of carved winged horses and cushioned in gold brocade.

His crown of gold and silver, too heavy to wear, was suspended above his head on fine golden chains. The food for his court was served on silver and gilt plates, exquisitely carved and chased, the wine from golden ewers, or from gold and silver rhytons—drinking horns in the animal-headed style still characteristic of the country.

One might expect attention to pleasure in such a setting, and indeed, it is found in a fourth-century Middle Persian text called *King Khosrow and His Knight*. In this tale, a youth named Vashpur presents himself to the greatest of Sasanian kings. Vashpur is well-born, well-schooled, skilled in the arts of war and peace alike, but his family has been ruined; he therefore asks King Khosrow to admit him to the royal court and volunteers for any test to prove his worth.

A plump partridge perching on a grapevine adorns a stucco plaque from the Sasanian palace of Eshqabad.

King Khosrow chooses to test the youth on his knowledge of cuisine (and of music, scents, women, and riding animals). Vashpur's answers provide hints of a very rarefied school of cookery, elements of which are recognizable in modern Iranian cuisine. Among the most savory of dishes, the youth says, is "the breast of a fat ox, which is well cooked in beef tea and eaten with sugar and sugar candy." Tender ragouts may be made from the hare, the entrails of a horse, or the head of a pheasant, but the best includes a young female gazelle. Among the best sweets are almond pastry and walnut pastry for summer, and almond and peach for winter, but the best dessert of all is a jelly made from the juice of the apple and the quince. The best shelled fruits include the coconut of India and Iran's own pistachios, and Vashpur praises dates stuffed with walnuts, pistachios, and peaches.

It might be thought that the conquest of Sasanian Persia by the Arab armies of Islam in 637 would end the rich civilization and the trade, for the desert warriors were rough men, who—according to the Persian poet Ferdowsi—fed on camel's milk and lizards. The Arabs reduced the palace of the Sasanian kings at Ctesiphon to rubble. They tore down the marble-floored throne room; they cut up the famous garden rug and sold the gems which had been attached to it. They melted down the treasures, including the golden ewers and rhytons and dishes, the silver forks and spoons; they scattered the vast libraries and burned the Persian texts. Then they moved on, hacking and burning their way through the cities of the Persian plateau and mountains.

What eventually happened, however, was that Persia civilized the Arabs. Within a few generations, the conquerors were building new cities in the circular style of the Sasanian Firuzabad; constructing buildings with the Sasanian vault dome, and courtyard; absorbing and extending Persian scholarship; writing poetry in a Persian language reborn and woven with Arabic; wearing Persian clothes; drinking Persian wine; and eating Persian food. Persia provided the model for the splendid centuries known as the Golden Age of Islam.

THE PLEASURES OF THE PALACE

The food of medieval Persia—descended from ancient styles, enriched and diversified by trade—was the parent of Persian cookery today. We know something about it from literature and something from a few rare early cookbooks.

One such cookbook was written in Baghdad in 1226 by Mohammad ibn al-Hasan ibn Mohammad al-Karim al-Katib al Baghdadi, a man devoted to his craft, as his preface announces: "Pleasures may be divided into six classes, to wit, food, drink, clothes, sex, scent, and sound. Of these, the noblest and most consequential is food, for food is the body's stay and the means of preserving life." While his book mentions kababs, his recipes focus on stew-like meat dishes (*khoresh*es). The herbs and spices are many of those we use today: coriander, cinnamon, ginger, cloves, mint, cumin, caraway, saffron. The sweet and sour and sweet and savory combinations, favored in Iran from ancient times, are the ancestors of those you will find in this book: Iranian cuisine emphasizes fruits, and many dishes combine fruits with meat. Sourness may come from pomegranates, limes, vinegar, sweetness comes from sweet fruits or juices, sugar, honey, and date syrup. This cook, as many before him, thickened his sauces with ground almonds and walnuts. Rice, although mentioned in some recipes, is given no special treatment in this early cookbook. The distinctive rice cookery of Iran was invented several hundred years later (see page 86).

In the interval, Iran suffered, along with half the world, the onslaughts of the Mongols—Chingis Khan, who liked to call himself "the flail of God," his grandson Hulagu, and a century later, Tamerlane. One would think that nothing could have survived them. So vast was the slaughter that it took more than 200 years for the Iranian population to reach pre-Mongol levels.

But Iran survived. Indeed, some of her arts thrived under Tamerlane's Persianized successors. It was during the thirteenth, fourteenth and fifteenth centuries that faience mosaic and miniature painting reached their peaks; it was then the great poets Rumi, Saadi, and Hafez worked.

And slowly out of the ruins rose the Safavid dynasty. Under them all the arts were reborn. The Safavids built Isfahan, "out of light itself," Victoria Sackville-West would write, "taking the turquoise of their sky, the green of spring trees, the yellow of the sun, the brown of the earth, the black of their sheep and turning these into solid light." This city of gardens, pavilions, palaces, and mosques glowed with the cosmopolitan spirit peculiar to Iran. Its greatest king, Shah Abbas, encouraged trade—including trade with the West—and cherished the civilized arts. He even brought in experts to improve Isfahan's reputedly inferior wine.

The sixteenth and seventeenth-century cuisine of the Safavids, in fact, was close to modern Iranian cookery, although the scale was unique. It was described by a visiting French Huguenot jeweler, Jean (Sir John) Chardin (whose enthusiastic reports on the culture of the Safavids were published in many volumes). Chardin reported carefully on all the customs of Iran: His account of a feast at Isfahan gives an idea of his style: "They served up the dinner after this manner: There were spread before all the company, cloths of gold brocade, and upon them, all along, there was bread of three or four sorts, very good, and well made: this done, they immediately brought eleven great basins of that sort of food called polow, which is rice baked with meat: There was of it, of all colors, and of all sorts of tastes, with sugar, with the juice of pomegranates, the juice of citrons, and with saffron: Each dish weighed above fourscore pounds, and had alone been sufficient to satisfy the whole assembly.... With these basins were served up four flat kettles.... One of them was full of eggs made into a pudding; another of soup with herbs [probably a herb *ash*]; another was filled with herbage and hashed meat [*kufteh*, page 62]; and the last with fried fish. All this being served upon the table, a porringer was set before each person, which was four times deeper than ours, filled with Sherbet of a tartish sweet taste, and a plate of winter and summer salads [probably fresh herbs and cheese]." The service, he added, no doubt from professional interest, was all of gold.

One of the Safavids' turbanned servants offers a tray of cooling sherbet, an antidote to summer's heat then as now. The image is a detail from a sixteenth century miniature.

Most of the recipes in this book would have been at home in Safavid Isfahan, although Iranian cookery has developed since then, of course, and added ingredients, such as tomatoes and potatoes from the New World. There are regional variations as well: People around the Caspian and on the Persian Gulf have their own styles of fish cookery, for instance. But certain basic themes remain. There are many yogurt-based dishes, called *borani* after a Sasanian queen who enjoyed them; these are a heritage, perhaps, of the centuries Iran shared a culture with western Asia. There is an emphasis on fruit, as might be expected from a country so rich in it. Fruit is often combined with meat, to make sweet and savory dishes or sweet and sour ones. Iranians love their distinctive rice dishes, their *chelows* and *polows*; in fact, we judge a cook's ability by them.

Besides that, Iranians share attitudes toward food. First, it is part of hospitality, which is central to Persian life. Hospitality must be generous: In traditional Persia, a host would remain standing, serving his guests and eating nothing himself. Customs change, but the attitude remains. Hospitality is like gift giving, the saying goes: One should do it handsomely or not at all.

Next, one should cook according to what is best in season, so that food is as fresh and of as good quality as may be. Fragrance, both during cooking and at the table, is almost as important as taste. And food should be presented handsomely, garnished so that it pleases the eye.

Then there is the ancient philosophy—linked in time and thought to the dualistic Zoroastrian religion of the Achaemenids and Sasanians—of hot and cold foods. It is a philosophy Iranians once shared with most of the civilized world, including China and India and the medieval West, where it was called the Salerno Regimen, after the city whose physicians taught it. It still affects the way foods are combined and served.

The philosophy rests on the belief that the body reflects the elements of earth, air, fire, and water in humors—blood, yellow bile, phlegm, and black bile. These should be in balance: If they are not, illness results. Proper diet is the way to bring the humors into balance. Foods are classified as hot, cold, wet, and dry, measurements not of temperature but of energy. Hot foods are high in it, cold foods low. The classifications vary from region to region, but generally speaking, animal fat, poultry, mutton, wheat, sugar, some fresh vegetables and fruits, and all dried vegetables and fruits are classified as hot; most beef, fish, dairy products, rice, and fresh vegetables and fruits are classified as cold. If you have a hot nature or a hot illness or it is summertime, you should be eating cold foods; if the weather is cool, or you have a cold ailment or a cold nature, you should be eating hot ones.

The everyday ideal, though, is balanced dishes, suitable to the occasion. That is one reason you will almost always find walnuts, a hot food, in dishes that include pomegranates, a cold one; or tart cherries with poultry. Another reason, of course, is that those ingredients taste absolutely wonderful together.

ON USING THIS BOOK

Please browse. You'll see that I have arranged the book in chapters on Appetizers, which include salads and dips, vegetables, soups, and the Iranian omelets called *kukus*; on Chicken, Meat and Fish; on Khoreshes, or scented stews; on Rice; and on Desserts. Every chapter has an introduction explaining what to expect in the recipes.

None of these recipes requires cooking techniques that are unusual or difficult to learn. To help in planning, I've listed preparation and cooking times for each dish, said whether it can be made in advance, and noted how many people it will serve.

Almost all the ingredients in the recipes are available at your local supermarket. Those that might not be or that require preliminary preparations are marked with an asterisk, which indicates that they are discussed in the Dictionary of Persian

Cookery on pages 160-70. Please do check—even read through—the dictionary: The entries describe the history of each ingredient and its use in Iran, and explain how to shop for it and how to prepare it. In many cases you will find substitutes for ingredients that seem exotic. These will work perfectly well; in one case—using low-cholesterol oil in place of the clarified butter of Iran—you may prefer them.

For most, however, I suggest you try to find the original. The Guide to Persian Groceries and Restaurants on pages 172-3 offers a comprehensive list of shops around the country that sell Iranian foods. With their help, you will be able to produce dishes with the authentic taste of Persia.

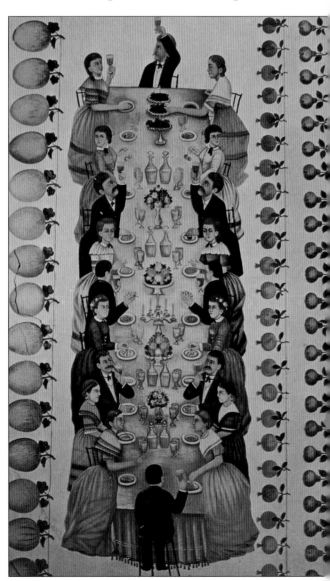

ON SHAPING MENUS

Planning an Iranian meal is simplicity itself. As you will see on page 24, all Iranian lunches and dinners begin with a range of appetizers, which always include bread, cheese, and fresh herbs, and may include salads and vegetables. The bread, cheese, and herbs stay on the table throughout the meal.

The rest of the meal may be as elaborate as you wish. For simple main courses, for instance, you might serve a *kuku* (pages 49–50) or a *khoresh* with *chelow* (pages 119–139) or *chelow-kabab* (page 54). Any of these, with Iranian appetizers and fruit for dessert, makes a delicious and balanced lunch or dinner. To elaborate, add one of the soups on page 40–48 and a dessert from the Desserts chapter.

For celebrations, you will think on a larger scale, and need more advance planning: As Jean Chardin observed, Iranian banquets are grand feasts of many dishes, all spread out buffet style. A wedding feast, for instance, would include (besides the usu-

al appetizers) at least one *kuku*; pistachio-stuffed lamb (page 66), meat or chicken kababs (pages 75-83); at least two rice dishes (one of them *Shirin Polow*, page 106, for sweetness); two *khoresh*es; a wedding cake; and a number of traditional sweets and pastries.

A nineteenth century Persian ceiling painting illustrates sharp contrasts between European and Iranian dining styles: For the hard-drinking Westerners, mixed company, voluminous clothes, and chairs around a table; for the Persians, a men's dinner, traditional formal clothes and floor cushions set around a fine cloth (sofreh).

The Persians, Herodotus remarked, were great wine drinkers. "It is also their general practice to deliberate upon affairs of weight when they are drunk; and then on the morrow, when they are sober, the decision to which they came the night before is put before them by the master of the house in which it was made; and if it is then approved of, they act on it; if not, they set it aside. Sometimes, however, they are sober at their first deliberation, but in this case they always reconsider the matter under the influence of wine." Wine is a recurring theme in classical Persian art and poetry:

Come fill the Cup, and in the fire of Spring
Your Winter-garment of Repentance fling
The Bird of Time has but a little way
To flutter—and the Bird is on the Wing

wrote Omar Khayyam, at least according to Edward FitzGerald, and he was not alone. Jean Chardin, who noticed everything, praised Safavid wine as the strongest in the world, and the most luscious.

In fact, the wine of Shiraz was famous. As it happens, Shiraz grapes, transported to Australia, are now producing excellent vintages, which would be appropriate with Persian food. In any case, for those who wish to drink wine, I suggest red wine—good Shirazes, Pinots or Cabernets—with the food in this book. The sole exception to the rule would be the wine of kings, Sauternes, if you can afford it. For those who do not wish to drink wine in this world, Islam promises a far more luscious wine in paradise.

Whatever you choose, you may raise a glass in the good wishes I now offer you. In Persian we say, NUSH!

On the facing page, a detail from a nineteenth century Persian painting, barefooted Zolaykha offers a glass of wine to her beloved Joseph. At her feet are figs and pomegranates. The drawing above is of a 500 BCE Achaemenid rhyton, a vessel with animal features, in this case a ram's head decorated around the rim with lotus flowers. From very ancient times Iranians used these vessels for drinking and ritual libations.

Appetizers

Yogurt & Cucumber Salad

Yogurt & Spinach Salad

Eggplant & Pomegranate Salad

Eggplant & Yogurt Dip

Lentil Dip

Cheese & Walnut Spread

Hot Fava Beans

Stuffed Quince

Stuffed Vegetables

Stuffed Grape Leaves

Noodle Soup

Cream of Barley

Pomegranate Soup

Pistachio Soup

Lamb Shank Soup

Yogurt Soup

Fresh Herb Kuku

Eggplant Kuku

*A*PPETIZERS

"That which I have admired very much in the way of living of the Persians, besides their sobriety, is their hospitality," wrote the inimitable Jean Chardin, in the seventeenth century. "When they eat, far from shutting the door, they give to every one about them, who happens to come at that time, and oftentimes to the servants who hold the horse at the gate. Let who will come at the dinner or supper-time, they are not the least put out of their way...."

Truly, hospitality is the soul of Persian cookery, and its symbol is appetizers. There are always many of them, so that whoever drops in (even the grooms at the gate) will feel welcomed by abundance. An Iranian first course—like its descendants, the *mezze* of Turkey, the *mezedes* of Greece, or the *tapas* of Spain—consists of a variety of little dishes to which people help themselves according to their fancy. In traditional houses, these dishes are arranged on a *sofreh*, a cotton cloth embroidered with poems or prayers that is spread over the carpet or table. Nowadays, it is easier to put them on a sideboard or on the table itself.

The general idea is to make the presentation inviting, pretty, and refreshing to the palate: Appetizers balance the dishes that make up the rest of a meal. To this end, a Persian table always provides *nan-o panir-o sabzi khordan*, which is to say, bread, cheese, and fresh vegetables and herbs. The bread may be any of the kinds described on page 160; the favorite is probably thin, crisp *lavash* bread, which you will find at the supermarket. The cheese, either cow's or goat's milk, should be fairly firm and white. You may wish to make your own (see page 161), but feta is a perfectly good substitute. As for the vegetables and herbs, offer crisp radishes and scallions, plus fresh coriander leaf (also known as cilantro), tarragon, mint, and basil—whatever is freshest and in season.

These are the basics, which stay on the table throughout the meal, Chardin observed. "They serve every one with two or three sorts of the leaf-bread, and an handful of strong herbs upon it to serve as a salad...." But possibilities for elaboration and variation are infinite, depending on your time, imagination, and number of guests. You may wish to add bowls of Persian pickles and relishes for a sharp contrast in flavor; you may wish to include other fresh vegetables and fruits such as peeled sliced cucumbers, melon slices, grapes, and shelled nuts and raisins. Salads range from simple mixtures of cucumbers, tomatoes, and onions with oil and vinegar to any of the compositions you will find on the following pages—mixtures of yogurt and vegetables, nuts and cheese, or eggplant or lentils with seasonings. All are simple to prepare and delicious to eat with *lavash* bread.

The first course is also the place for cooked vegetables. Iranians rarely serve vegetables as side dishes to a main course, as in the West: Most main courses contain vegetables in any case. There are, however, many vegetable dishes suitable for first courses. Among them are steamed beets—a favorite in Iran—and cooked, seasoned beans. Then there are stuffed vine leaves, eggplants, tomatoes, apples, and quinces, which are served cold as appetizers or hot as main courses.

The same may be said for the baked omelets known as *kuku*s. These, good hot or cold, are often kept on hand in the refrigerator to serve as snacks or appetizers for unexpected guests.

And then there are soups, or *ashe*s, best made a day in advance so that their flavors have time to meld. Some, like Pistachio Soup (page 45) or Cream of Barley Soup (page 42), are so light and elegant they make excellent preliminaries for main courses to follow: Serve them individually, after people have had a chance to try the other appetizers. Other *ashe*s, such as Pomegranate Soup (page 44) or Noodle Soup (page 40), might be main courses in themselves, especially on a cold winter's day.

Yogurt & Cucumber Salad

Mast-o khiar

SERVINGS: *4*
PREP TIME: *15 min. plus 15 min. refrigeration*
COOKING TIME: *none*

1 long seedless or
  seeded cucumber,
  peeled and diced
3 cups plain low-fat or
  whole yogurt
¼ cup chopped scallions
2 tablespoons chopped
  fresh mint
2 tablespoons chopped
  fresh dill
2 tablespoons chopped
  fresh oregano, or ½
  teaspoon dried
1 tablespoon chopped
  fresh thyme, or ½
  teaspoon dried
4 tablespoons chopped
  fresh tarragon, or ½
  teaspoon dried
2 cloves garlic, peeled
  and crushed
3 tablespoons chopped
  walnuts
1 teaspoon salt
1 teaspoon freshly
  ground black pepper
½ cup raisins, washed
  and drained

GARNISH
Sprigs of fresh mint
Sprigs of fresh dill
3 tablespoons dried rose
  petals
2 tablespoons raisins
2 tablespoons chopped
  walnuts
1 radish, diced

In summer, this salad is frequently transformed into a wonderfully refreshing cold soup, called Abdugh khiar *in Persian, by adding 1 cup of croutons or crumbled, toasted* lavash *bread, 2 or 3 ice cubes and cold water to create a soup of the preferred consistency. My husband doubles the raisin quantity and adds a whole cup of water to make his a very thin soup that can be sipped straight from a bowl or cup.*

1. In a serving bowl, combine all the ingredients except the raisins. Mix thoroughly and adjust seasoning. The raisins may be added now, but they will absorb liquid and become plump and soft instead of chewy.

2. Refrigerate for at least 15 minutes, or up to 4 hours, before serving. If the salad is refrigerated for more than an hour, remove it from the refrigerator 10 minutes before serving. Just prior to serving add the raisins and mix thoroughly.

3. Garnish with the mint, rose petals, raisins, and walnuts and serve with *lavash* bread. NUSH-E JAN!

Yogurt & Spinach Salad

Borani-e esfenaj

SERVINGS: 4
PREP TIME: 10 min. plus
15 min. refrigeration
COOKING TIME: 30 min.

2 tablespoons vegetable
  oil, butter, or ghee*
2 onions, peeled and
  thinly sliced
2 cloves garlic, peeled
  and crushed
5 cups washed and
  chopped fresh spinach
  (about 12 ounces), or
  1½ cups frozen
  spinach, thawed
1½ cups drained
  yogurt*
½ teaspoon salt
½ teaspoon freshly
  ground black pepper

GARNISH (optional)
½ teaspoon ground
  saffron threads,*
  dissolved in 1
  tablespoon hot water
1 tablespoon dried rose
  petals

Borani *recipes are named for the fourth-century Sasanian queen, Pouran* dokht. Queen Pourandokht was fond of yogurt, and her chef made her many dishes with drained yogurt and vegetables. These dishes were called Pourani after her, and in time Pourani became Borani.

1. In a large skillet heat the oil over medium heat. Add the onions and garlic and fry for 20 minutes, stirring occasionally to prevent burning, until the onions are soft and brown.

2. Add the spinach, cover, and steam 5 to 10 minutes, until the spinach is wilted.

3. Remove from heat and let cool for 10 to 15 minutes; transfer to a serving bowl.

4. Add the yogurt, salt and pepper. Refrigerate for at least 15 minutes, or up to 8 hours, before serving. If the salad is refrigerated for more than an hour, remove it from the refrigerator 10 minutes before serving.

5. Garnish with saffron water and rose petals or any other edible flower. Serve with *lavash* bread. NUSH-E JAN!

Eggplant & Pomegranate Salad

Nazkhatun

SERVINGS: *4*
PREP TIME: *15 min.*
COOKING TIME: *1½ hours*

- 3 medium eggplants (about 2 pounds)
- 3 tablespoons olive oil
- 2 medium onions, peeled and thinly sliced
- 2 cloves garlic, peeled and crushed
- 4 medium tomatoes, peeled* and thinly sliced
- 2 tablespoons pomegranate paste*
- 1 teaspoon salt
- ½ teaspoon freshly ground black pepper
- 1 teaspoon angelica powder*
- ½ cup chopped fresh mint or 2 teaspoons dried

1. Preheat the oven to 350°F. Rinse the eggplant and prick it in several places with a fork to prevent bursting.

2. Place the eggplant on the center rack of the oven, with a baking sheet underneath the rack to catch the drippings. Bake for 1 hour. A more traditional cooking method is to grill the eggplant for about 40 minutes, turning frequently, over a charcoal or wood fire that has burned down to embers.

3. Remove the eggplant from the oven, place it on a cutting board, and let it stand until cool enough to handle. Remove the eggplant skin with your hands and chop the flesh.

4. In a large skillet heat the oil over medium heat. Add the onions and garlic, and fry for 20 minutes, stirring occasionally to prevent burning. Add the tomatoes and pomegranate paste and stir-fry for another 10 minutes.

5. Add the eggplant, salt, pepper, angelica powder, and mint. Stirring occasionally, simmer over low heat 25 to 35 minutes until the mixture is thick. Adjust seasoning to taste.

6. Transfer to a serving dish and serve hot or cold with *lavash* bread. This recipe may be made up to 4 hours in advance. If the salad is refrigerated for more than an hour, remove it from the refrigerator 10 minutes before serving. NUSH-E JAN!

Eggplant & Yogurt Dip

Borani-e bademjan

SERVINGS: *4*
PREP TIME: *15 min.*
COOKING TIME: *1 hour*

2 large eggplants (about
  2 pounds)
1 tablespoon olive oil
4 cloves garlic, peeled
  and crushed
1 teaspoon salt
½ teaspoon freshly
  ground black pepper
⅔ cup drained yogurt*
4 tablespoons chopped
  fresh mint or 1
  teaspoon dried
2 tablespoons fresh lime
  juice

GARNISH
¼ teaspoon ground
  saffron threads ,*
  dissolved in 2
  tablespoons hot water
  (optional)
1 tablespoon drained
  yogurt*
Fresh mint leaves

1. Preheat the oven to 350°F. Rinse the eggplant and prick it in several places with a fork to prevent bursting.

2. Place the eggplant in the center rack of the oven, with a baking sheet underneath the rack to catch the drippings. Bake for 1 hour. A more traditional cooking method is to grill the eggplant for about 40 minutes, turning frequently, over a charcoal or wood fire that has burned down to embers.

3. Remove the eggplant from the oven, place it on a cutting board, and let it stand until cool enough to handle. Remove the eggplant skin with your hands and chop the flesh.

4. Transfer the flesh to a mixing bowl, add the remaining ingredients, and mix thoroughly. Adjust seasoning to taste.

5. Transfer to a serving dish, garnish with saffron water, drained yogurt, and mint leaves and serve hot or cold with *lavash* bread. This recipe may be made up to 24 hours in advance and stored in the refrigerator. If the dip is refrigerated for more than an hour, remove it from the refrigerator 10 minutes before serving. *NUSH-E JAN!*

Lentil Dip

Adasi

SERVINGS: *6*
PREP TIME: *15 min.*
COOKING TIME: *1¼ hours*

2 cups green lentils, picked over and washed
3 tablespoons vegetable oil, butter, or ghee*
2 large onions, peeled and thinly sliced
4 cloves garlic, peeled and crushed
1 teaspoon salt
½ teaspoon freshly ground black pepper
1 tablespoon angelica powder*
½ cup Seville orange juice* or a mixture of 2 tablespoons fresh lime juice and ¼ cup fresh orange juice

1. Place the lentils in a large saucepan and add 6 cups of water and 1 teaspoon of salt. Bring to a boil.

2. Cover and simmer over low heat for about 30 minutes, stirring occasionally; add more water as necessary to keep the beans immersed.

3. In a large skillet heat the oil over medium heat. Add onions and garlic and fry for 20 minutes, stirring occasionally to prevent burning.

4. Add the fried onion mixture, salt, and pepper to the lentils and bring to a boil. Cover and simmer over low heat for another 45 minutes.

5. Add angelica powder and Seville orange juice and adjust seasonings to taste. Serve hot or cold with *lavash* bread. This recipe may be made up to 24 hours in advance and stored in the refrigerator. If the salad is refrigerated for more than an hour, remove it from the refrigerator 10 minutes before serving. *NUSH-E JAN!*

Cheese & Walnut Spread

Nan-o panir-o-gerdu

SERVINGS: *2*

PREP TIME: *15 min.*

COOKING TIME: *none*

¼ pound feta cheese
2 cups chopped walnuts
¼ cup fresh scallions
¼ cup fresh basil
¼ cup fresh tarragon
¼ cup fresh mint
1 clove garlic, peeled
   and crushed
½ teaspoon salt
¼ teaspoon freshly
   ground black pepper
1 tablespoon fresh lime
   juice
¼ cup olive oil

To measure the quantities called for in this recipe, first chop the herbs. Traditionally, the herbs are chopped by hand, resulting in a coarser textured spread.

1. In a food processor, mix all the ingredients to create a grainy paste. Taste and adjust seasoning.

2. Transfer the mixture to a serving bowl and place on a round platter.

3. Cut *lavash* or pita bread into 4-inch pieces and arrange around the bowl on a platter. You can also use sliced and toasted French or Italian bread. NUSH-E JAN!

Hot Fava Beans

Baqala pokhteh

SERVINGS: *4*
PREP TIME: *1 min.*
COOKING TIME: *15 min.*

2 pounds fresh fava
   beans in the pod, or 1
   pound frozen fava
   beans*
¼ cup salt
¼ cup red wine vinegar
2 teaspoons angelica
   powder*

Hot fava beans are a popular snack, and vendors are a familiar sight in Iranian towns and cities, much like chestnut vendors in winter in New York. The beans also make a nice addition to a table of appetizers. Baqala pokhteh *is traditionally prepared with fresh fava beans in the pod and eaten much as one would eat peanuts in the shell; however, if you can't find them, use frozen beans.*

1. Rinse the fresh beans but do not shell them. Frozen beans are already shelled.

2. In a large pot, bring 5 quarts of water and ¼ cup of salt to a boil.

3. Add the fresh beans and boil briskly for 10 to 15 minutes. Boil frozen beans only 5 minutes, or until tender.

4. Drain the beans, transfer them to a platter, sprinkle with the vinegar and angelica powder, and serve. If using fresh fava beans in the pod, shell them as you eat them. NUSH-E-JAN!

Stuffed Quince

Dolmeh-ye beh

SERVINGS: *4*
PREP TIME: *45 min.*
COOKING TIME: *1½ hours*

4 medium quince
½ cup brown sugar
4 tablespoons vegetable
   oil, butter, or ghee*
1 onion, peeled and
   thinly sliced
½ pound lean ground
   beef, lamb, or chicken
¼ cup long-grain rice
1 teaspoon salt
½ teaspoon freshly
   ground black pepper
1 teaspoon Persian spice
   mix (*advieh*)*
1 cup apple juice or beef
   broth*
¼ cup balsamic vinegar
¼ cup fresh lime juice
¼ teaspoon ground
   saffron threads,*
   dissolved in 1
   tablespoon hot water
   (optional)

1. Wash the quince and rub off the fuzz. Cut off the tops and set them aside. Hollow out the quince, using the tip of a knife or a melon-baller to scoop out the seeds and some of the pulp, leaving a shell about ½-inch thick. Reserve the pulp. Sprinkle 1 teaspoon brown sugar into each quince shell.

2. In a large skillet, heat 2 tablespoons of oil over medium heat. Add the onion and meat and fry for 15 minutes, stirring occasionally, until golden brown. Add the rice, salt, pepper, and *advieh* and stir-fry 1 minute.

3. Add ½ cup water and bring to a boil. Reduce the heat to low, cover, and simmer for 15 minutes.

4. Fill each quince with stuffing, replace the tops, and arrange the quince side by side in a deep, lidded pan. Add the apple juice and the quince pulp to the pan and pour 2 tablespoons of oil over the stuffed quince. Place 2 layers of paper towel over the pan and cover tightly with the lid. Be careful that the paper towels do not burn. Simmer over low heat for 1 hour.

5. In a saucepan, combine the vinegar, lime juice, remaining brown sugar, and saffron water, and bring to a boil. Pour this mixture over the stuffed quince, cover, and cook for another 30 minutes.

6. Adjust seasonings to taste with sugar or vinegar, and check to see whether the fruit is tender. If it isn't, cook another 15 minutes. Serve in the same dish or on a platter with bread, yogurt, and fresh herbs. NUSH-E JAN!

Variation: Stuffed Apples

You can replace the quince with baking apples. Instead of cooking on top of the stove, cover and bake the hollowed-out apples in a preheated 350°F oven for 30 minutes. Remove them from the oven, add the mixture from Step 4, return to the oven, and bake uncovered for another 30 minutes.

Stuffed Peppers, Eggplants & Tomatoes

Dolmeh-ye felfel sabz-o bademjan-o gojeh farangi

SERVINGS: *4–6*
PREP TIME: *1 hour*
COOKING TIME: *1¼ hours*

2 round eggplants*
2 green bell peppers
4 large tomatoes
½ cup vegetable oil,
    butter, or ghee*
¼ cup long-grain rice
¼ cup yellow split peas*
2¼ teaspoons salt
1 onion, peeled and
    thinly sliced
2 cloves garlic, peeled
    and crushed
1 pound lean ground
    beef, lamb, or veal
2 tablespoons tomato
    paste
1 cup chopped fresh
    parsley
½ cup chopped chives
    or scallions
1 cup chopped fresh
    mint or 1 tablespoon
    dried
1 cup chopped fresh
    tarragon or 1
    tablespoon dried
½ teaspoon freshly
    ground black pepper
½ teaspoon Persian
    spice mix (*advieh*)*
1 cup tomato juice
⅓ cup fresh lime juice
    or red wine vinegar
½ cup sugar
1 teaspoon ground
    cinnamon
¼ teaspoon ground
    saffron threads,*
    dissolved in 2
    tablespoons hot water

PREPARING THE SHELLS

1. Cut off the stem ends of the eggplants and set aside. Slice off the bottoms so the shells will stand upright. Using the point of a knife or a melon-baller, remove the flesh, leaving shells about ¾-inch thick. Discard the flesh. Peel the shells, sprinkle them inside and out with 1 tablespoon salt, and place them in a colander to drain for 20 minutes. Rinse them and pat them dry. Then brown the shells on all sides in 3 tablespoons of oil in a skillet set over medium heat, adding oil as necessary if the pan dries out. This takes about 10 minutes. Set the shells aside to drain on paper towels.

2. Cut off the tops of the green peppers ½-inch from the stems and set the tops aside. Remove the seeds and ribs from the peppers. Blanch the peppers and tops for 5 minutes in boiling water. Rinse in cold water and drain.

3. Remove the stems from the tomatoes. Cut off the tops and set aside. With a melon-baller, scoop out the pulp and reserve it.

MAKING THE STUFFING

1. In a small pot, combine the rice, split peas, 2 cups water, and ¼ teaspoon salt, and bring to a boil. Reduce the heat to medium, cover, and simmer for 20 minutes. Remove from heat, drain and set aside.

2. In a large skillet, heat 2 tablespoons oil over medium heat. Add onions, garlic, and meat and fry for 15 minutes, stirring occasionally, until golden brown. Add the tomato paste, stir-fry 1 minute, and remove the pan from the heat.

3. Add the rice mixture and the parsley, chives, mint, and tarragon to the meat. Season with 1 teaspoon salt, ½ teaspoon pepper, ½ teaspoon *advieh* and mix thoroughly.

BAKING THE STUFFING

1. Preheat the oven to 400°F.

2. Fill the eggplants, tomatoes, and green peppers with the stuffing and replace their tops.

3. Place the stuffed eggplants and peppers side by side in an ovenproof dish, leaving room for the tomatoes, which will be added later.

4. In a saucepan combine the reserved tomato pulp, tomato juice, 2 tablespoons of oil, lime juice, sugar, cinnamon, 1 teaspoon salt and the saffron water. Pour this mixture around the stuffed vegetables. Cover and bake in the preheated oven for 50 minutes.

5. Remove the dish from the oven, uncover it, and add the stuffed tomatoes. Cover and return to the oven. Bake for 30 to 45 minutes, or until the vegetables are tender.

6. When the vegetables are done, taste the sauce and adjust the lime juice, sugar, or salt as needed. Serve in the baking dish or on a platter with bread and yogurt. NUSH-E JAN!

Variation: **Stuffed Potatoes**

Whole potatoes are also excellent for stuffing. Peel them and use a melon-baller to dig out circular sections to form a shell. Stuff and bake about 1 hour along with the sauce as directed for the other vegetables.

Variation: **Stuffed Onions**

Whole peeled, cored onions are also excellent for stuffing. Core them and use a melon-baller to dig circular sections to form a shell. Blanch the shells in boiling water for 1 minute and drain before stuffing. Bake about 1½ hours at 375°F in a baking pan along with the sauce as directed for other vegetables.

Stuffed Grape Leaves

Dolmeh-ye barg-e mo

SERVINGS: 6 8
PREP TIME: *1 hour*
COOKING TIME: *1 hour*

50 fresh grape leaves in
    season or 1 16-ounce
    jar canned leaves*
⅔ cup long-grain rice
¼ cup yellow split peas*
1 teaspoon salt
½ cup vegetable oil,
    butter, or ghee*
1 onion, peeled and
    thinly sliced
2 cloves garlic, peeled
    and crushed
½ pound lean ground
    beef, lamb, or chicken
1 cup chopped scallions
¼ cup chopped fresh
    summer savory or 1
    tablespoon dried
½ cup chopped fresh
    dill or 2 tablespoons
    dried
¼ cup chopped fresh
    tarragon or 1
    tablespoon dried
¼ cup chopped fresh
    mint or 1 tablespoon
    dried
3½ cups chopped fresh
    parsley or 1 cup dried
1 teaspoon freshly
    ground black pepper
1 teaspoon ground
    cinnamon
1 cup beef broth*
⅔ cup sugar
⅓ cup red wine vinegar
⅓ cup fresh lemon or
    lime juice

1. If you are using fresh grape leaves, pick small and tender ones. Blanch, drain and rinse them.* Drain canned grape leaves in a colander and rinse under cold running water.

2. In a small saucepan, combine the rice, split peas, 3 cups water, and ½ teaspoon salt, and bring to a boil. Reduce the heat to medium and simmer for 15 minutes. Drain and set aside.

3. In a large skillet, heat 3 tablespoons oil over medium heat. Add the onions, garlic, and meat and fry for 15 minutes, stirring occasionally, until golden brown. Add the rice mixture, scallions, chopped herbs, pepper, cinnamon, and ½ teaspoon salt. Mix thoroughly with a wooden spoon and adjust seasoning to taste.

4. Place three layers of grape leaves on the bottom of a well-oiled ovenproof dish. Preheat the oven to 400°F.

5. Place a grape leaf, vein side up, on a wooden board and nip off the stem. Top with 1 tablespoon of stuffing. Roll up the leaf, folding in the ends to prevent the stuffing from leaking. Place in the dish on top of the grape-leaf base. Repeat, filling all the remaining leaves.

6. Pour the broth and the remaining oil over the stuffed grape leaves. Set a small ovenproof plate on top to keep them from unfolding. Cover and bake in the oven for 30 minutes.

7. Mix the sugar, vinegar, and lime juice. Remove the baking dish from the oven, uncover the grape leaves, and baste with this mixture. Cover and return to the oven to bake for 30 minutes.

8. When the grape leaves are tender, taste the sauce and adjust seasoning. The sauce should be quite reduced. Serve in the baking dish or on a platter, while hot or warm, with bread and yogurt. *NUSH-E JAN!*

Noodle Soup

Ash-e reshteh

SERVINGS: *6*
PREP TIME: *20 min.*
COOKING TIME: *2 hours*

¼ cup dried chickpeas
¼ cup dried navy beans
¼ cup dried red kidney
  beans
3 tablespoons vegetable
  oil, butter, or ghee*
3 large onions, peeled
  and thinly sliced
5 cloves garlic, peeled
  and crushed
2 teaspoons salt
½ teaspoon freshly
  ground black pepper
1 teaspoon ground
  turmeric
10 cups water
1 cup green lentils
4 cups beef broth*
½ pound dry Persian
  noodles,* broken in
  half, or linguine
1 tablespoon all-
  purpose flour
1 cup coarsely chopped
  fresh chives or
  scallions
1 cup chopped fresh dill
2 cups coarsely chopped
  fresh parsley
10 cups washed and
  chopped fresh spinach
  (about 6 pounds
  unchopped), or 3
  pounds frozen
  spinach, chopped
1 fresh beet, peeled and
  diced in ½-inch pieces
1½ cup liquid whey,* or
  sour cream, or ¼ cup
  wine vinegar

Some historians say that noodles originated in Persia and not China. They are mentioned in thirteenth-century Persian poems and shown in fifteenth-century illustrations. In Iran they are traditionally served on Nowruz, *the Iranian New Year, when eating them symbolizes unraveling the difficulties of the year to come. Another traditional occasion is on the third day after friends and relatives have gone away on a trip. It is believed that by eating noodles we can send the travelers luck as they follow the path of their journey. For best results, make your soup a day in advance to give the flavors a chance to meld; reheat it just before serving. Add the garnish at the last minute, after pouring the soup into the tureen.*

1. Soak the chickpeas, navy beans, and kidney beans in 4 cups of water for at least two hours. Drain and set aside.

2. In a large, heavy pot heat the oil over medium heat. Add the onions and garlic and fry for 15 minutes, stirring occasionally, until golden brown. Add the salt, pepper, turmeric, kidney beans, navy beans, and chickpeas; stir-fry for 1 minute.

3. Add 10 cups of water and bring to a boil. Reduce the heat to medium, cover partially, and simmer for 45 minutes.

4. Add the lentils and beef broth. Cook 20 minutes longer.

5. Add the noodles and flour and cook about 10 minutes, stirring occasionally.

6. Add the chopped chives, dill, parsley, spinach, and the beet. Continue cooking, stirring occasionally for 30 minutes, or until the beans are tender. Add salt and pepper to taste, and add more water if the soup is too thick.

7. Meanwhile, prepare the garnish in a skillet set over medium heat. Heat 1 tablespoon oil, add 1 peeled and sliced onion and fry for 15 minutes, stirring occasionally. Add 6 cloves peeled and crushed garlic and stir-fry until golden brown. Remove from the heat, add 1 teaspoon ground turmeric and 4 tablespoons crushed, dried mint, mix well, and set aside.

8. Stir the whey into the soup, saving a dollop for the garnish, and mix well with a wooden spoon.

9. Pour the soup into a tureen or individual serving bowls. Garnish with a dollop of whey and the garnish prepared in Step 7. NUSH-E JAN!

Cream of Barley

Soup-e jow

SERVINGS. *6*
PREP TIME: *20 min.*
COOKING TIME: *2 hours*

2 tablespoons vegetable oil, butter, or ghee*
2 onions, peeled and thinly sliced
2 cloves garlic, peeled and crushed
1 carrot, peeled and grated
3 leeks, finely chopped
4 cups water
½ cup barley
1 teaspoon salt
½ teaspoon freshly ground black pepper
3 cups beef or chicken broth*
½ cup sour cream
Juice of 1 lime or lemon

GARNISH
2 tablespoons chopped fresh parsley
½ teaspoon freshly ground black pepper

In Persian cuisine, soups are lighter than ashes. Soups are best served as appetizers for complex meals; ashes should be served as appetizers for simple dishes such as kababs or chickpea patties, or they may be meals unto themselves.

1. In a large pot heat the oil over medium heat. Add the onions and garlic and fry 15 minutes, stirring occasionally, until golden brown. Add the carrot and the leeks and stir-fry 1 minute.

2. Add the water, barley, salt, and pepper. Bring to a boil, reduce the heat to low, cover, and simmer for 1 hour, stirring occasionally, or until the barley is tender.

3. Add the broth, cover, and simmer over low heat for 30 to 40 minutes. Using a slotted spoon, transfer the solid ingredients to a blender. Add the sour cream and lime juice to them and blend thoroughly. Return the purée to the pot.

4. Bring the soup to a boil, reduce the heat, and correct seasoning to taste, adding salt, pepper, or lime juice as needed. If the soup is too thick, add more warm water. Continue simmering for another 5 minutes over low heat.

5. Just before serving, pour the soup into a tureen or individual serving bowls. Garnish the soup with black pepper, parsley, or a sprig of oregano. NUSH-E JAN!

Pomegranate Soup

Ash-e anar

SERVINGS: 6
PREP TIME: *20 min.*
COOKING TIME: *1¾ hours*

3 tablespoons vegetable oil, butter, or ghee*
4 medium onions (3 peeled and thinly sliced, 1 peeled and grated)
3 cloves garlic, peeled and crushed
½ cup yellow split peas*
8 cups water
1¼ teaspoons salt
½ teaspoon freshly ground black pepper
1 teaspoon ground turmeric
2⅛ cups chopped fresh parsley
2 cups chopped fresh coriander (cilantro)
1 cup chopped fresh mint or 2 tablespoons dried
2 cups chopped fresh chives or scallions
1 beet, peeled and chopped
½ pound lean ground beef, veal, or lamb
1 cup long-grain rice
⅔ cup pomegranate paste diluted in 2 cups of water, or 4 cups pomegranate juice, or 4 cups fresh pomegranate seeds*
⅓ cup sugar
2 tablespoons angelica powder*
1 tablespoon angelica seeds

For best results, make your soup a day in advance to give the flavors a chance to meld; reheat it just before serving. Add the garnish at the last minute, after pouring the soup into the tureen.

1. In a large, heavy pot heat the oil over medium heat. Add 3 sliced onions and the garlic and fry about 20 minutes, stirring occasionally, until golden brown. Add the split peas and stir-fry 1 minute longer.

2. Add 8 cups water. Bring to boil, reduce heat, partially cover, and simmer over medium heat for 20 minutes.

3. Add 1 teaspoon salt, ¼ teaspoon pepper; the turmeric; 2 cups of parsley; the coriander, mint, chives; and the beet. Continue cooking for 20 minutes longer, stirring occasionally with a wooden spoon to prevent sticking.

4. Combine the grated onion and the meat in a bowl. Season with ¼ teaspoon salt, ¼ teaspoon pepper, and 2 tablespoons chopped parsley. Mix the ingredients thoroughly. Shape the mixture into chestnut-size meatballs, and add them to the pot.

5. Add the rice, partially cover, and cook for 30 minutes longer.

6. Stir in the diluted pomegranate paste, sugar, and angelica powder, and simmer over low heat for 15 minutes.

7. Check a meatball: It should be cooked through. Taste the soup for seasoning: It should be sweet and sour. Add sugar if it is too sour, pomegranate paste if it is too sweet. Add warm water if the soup is too thick.

8. Just before serving, prepare the garnish. In a skillet, heat 1 tablespoon of oil over medium heat, add 5 cloves peeled and crushed garlic, and stir-fry until golden brown. Remove from heat and add 2 tablespoons dried mint and ½ teaspoon ground turmeric and mix well.

9. Pour the warmed soup into a tureen and garnish with the mint and garlic mixture, 2 tablespoons pomegranate seeds, and 1 tablespoon angelica seeds. NUSH-E JAN!

Pistachio Soup

Soup-e pesteh

SERVINGS: *4*
PREP TIME: *10 min.*
COOKING TIME: *55 min.*

1 cup unsalted blanched
   pistachios, almonds,
   or hazelnuts
1 tablespoon olive oil
1 shallot, chopped
2 leeks, chopped
1 clove garlic, peeled
   and crushed
2 tablespoons rice
   flour*
6 cups chicken broth*
1 teaspoon salt
¼ teaspoon pepper
½ cup Seville orange
   juice or a mixture of 2
   tablespoons fresh lime
   juice and ¼ cup fresh
   orange juice*

GARNISH
¼ cup whole unsalted
   pistachios or
   barberries, cleaned*

The word "pistachio" comes from the Persian word pesteh *and one ancient nickname for the Persian people was "pistachio-eaters." According to a Greek chronicler, when King Astyages of the Medes gazed from his throne over his army, which had been defeated by Cyrus the Great, he exclaimed, "Woe, how brave are these pistachio-eating Persians!"*

1. Grind the pistachios in a food processor or grinder.

2. In a heavy pot, heat the oil over medium heat. Add the shallot and leeks, and stir-fry for 5 minutes, until translucent. Add the garlic and stir-fry 3 minutes.

3. Add the rice flour, stirring constantly with a wooden spoon. Add the chicken broth and bring to a boil.

4. Add the pistachios, salt, and pepper, and reduce the heat to low. Cover and simmer for 45 minutes, stirring occasionally.

5. Add the Seville orange juice. Adjust seasoning to taste.

6. Pour the soup into a tureen or individual serving bowls, garnish with pistachios or barberries, and serve hot or cold. NUSH-E JAN!

Lamb Shank Soup

Abgusht-e lapeh-o gusht-e kubideh

SERVINGS: *6*
PREP TIME: *10 min.*
COOKING TIME: *2¼ hours*

2 pounds lamb shanks and 1 pound breast of lamb, bone-in
2 large onions, peeled and quartered
6–8 cups water
1 cup yellow split peas*
1 teaspoon ground turmeric
2 teaspoons salt
½ teaspoon freshly ground black pepper
3 large potatoes, peeled and cut into halves
4 tomatoes, peeled and sliced
1 tablespoon tomato paste
2 teaspoons ground cinnamon
4 whole dried Persian limes,* pierced, or ¼ cup lime juice
½ teaspoon ground saffron threads,* dissolved in 2 tablespoons hot water
1 teaspoon Persian spice mix (*advieh*)*

GARNISH
1 large onion, peeled and sliced
1 teaspoon ground cinnamon

1. Place the meat, onion, and 6 cups of water in a large pot. Bring to a boil, skimming the froth as it forms. Add split peas, turmeric, salt, and pepper. Cover and let simmer for 1½ hours over low heat.

2. Add the potatoes, tomatoes, tomato paste, cinnamon, limes, saffron water, *advieh*, and more water if necessary. Continue to simmer 45 minutes over low heat.

3. Test with a fork to see if the meat and potatoes are tender. Adjust seasoning to taste.

4. Using a slotted spoon, remove all of the stew ingredients. Debone the meat and reserve the bones. Mash the meat and vegetables together to make the paste called *gusht kubideh*. It should have the consistency of lumpy mashed potatoes. Iranian cooks would use a mortar and pestle to pound the *gusht kubideh* to just the right consistency. A food processor may be used instead, but take care not to let the paste get too smooth.

5. Season to taste with salt and pepper and arrange on a serving platter. Pour 3 tablespoons hot soup over the paste. Sprinkle with cinnamon and garnish with fresh onion and herbs.

6. Scoop out the marrow from the bones, add to the broth and reheat. Serve in a bowl as soup with the *gusht kubideh* on the side with Persian pickles (*torshi*), a platter of spring onions, radishes, fresh tarragon, basil, and mint (*sabzi-khordan*) and *lavash* or pita bread. NUSH-E JAN!

Yogurt Soup

Ash-e mast

SERVINGS: *6*
PREP TIME: *10 min.*
COOKING TIME: *1¾ hours*

¼ cup vegetable oil, butter, or ghee*
3 large onions, 2 peeled and thinly sliced, 1 peeled and grated
2 teaspoons salt
½ teaspoon freshly ground black pepper
½ teaspoon ground turmeric
½ cup dried chickpeas or yellow split peas
½ cup green lentils
8 cups water
½ pound lean ground beef
1 cup and 2 tablespoons chopped fresh parsley or ¼ cup dried
1 cup long-grain rice
2 cups chopped fresh coriander (cilantro) or ½ cup dried
½ cup chopped fresh chives or scallions or 2 tablespoons dried
3 sprigs fresh tarragon
1 cup chopped fresh dill or ¼ cup dried
1 cup fresh fenugreek or 2 tablespoons dried
4 cups washed and chopped fresh spinach (about 3 pounds), or 1 cup frozen spinach, chopped
3 turnips, chopped
3 cups plain yogurt

This soup is an excellent remedy for cold symptoms. For best results, make it a day in advance to give the flavors a chance to meld and reheat it just before serving. Add the garnish at the last minute, after pouring the soup into the tureen.

1. In a large pot, heat the oil over medium heat. Add 2 sliced onions and fry for 15 minutes, stirring occasionally, or until golden brown. Add 1½ teaspoons salt, ¼ teaspoon pepper, and the turmeric. Add the chickpeas and lentils and stir-fry 1 minute.

2. Add 8 cups of water and bring to a boil. Reduce heat to medium, partially cover, and simmer for 35 minutes.

3. Meanwhile, combine the grated onion with the meat in a bowl. Season with ½ teaspoon salt, ¼ teaspoon pepper, and 2 tablespoons parsley. Mix, shape into chestnut-sized meatballs, and set aside.

4. Add the rice to the pot and bring the mixture back to a boil. Add the meatballs and simmer partially covered 25 minutes longer.

5. Add the chopped herbs, spinach, and turnips and cook another 30 minutes, stirring occasionally.

6. Check to see that the chickpeas are tender and adjust seasoning to taste.

7. Prepare the garnish in a skillet, heating 2 tablespoons oil over medium heat. Add 1 peeled and sliced onion and 10 cloves peeled and crushed garlic and fry 15 minutes, stirring occasionally, until golden brown. Remove the skillet from heat, add ½ teaspoon turmeric and 2 tablespoons dried mint. Mix well, and set aside.

8. Stir a few spoonfuls of hot soup into the yogurt, blend well, and add to the pot, stirring clockwise constantly for 5 minutes to prevent curdling. Do not allow the soup to come to a boil.

9. Pour the hot soup into a tureen or individual serving bowls. Garnish with the mint mixture and serve with *lavash* or pita bread. *NUSH-E JAN!*

Variation: You may substitute ½ pound giblets for the ground beef. In this case, brown the sliced onions and giblets together in Step 1.

Fresh Herb Kuku
Kuku-ye sabzi

SERVINGS: *4*
PREP TIME: *25 min.*
COOKING TIME: *45 min.*

½ cup vegetable oil, butter, or ghee*

5 eggs

1 teaspoon baking powder

2 teaspoons Persian spice mix (*advieh*)*

1 teaspoon salt

1 teaspoon freshly ground black pepper

2 cloves garlic, peeled and crushed

1 cup chopped fresh garlic, chives, or leeks

1 cup chopped fresh parsley

1 cup chopped fresh coriander (cilantro)

1 cup chopped fresh dill

1 tablespoon all-purpose flour

1 tablespoon dried fenugreek or 2 tablespoons dried barberries, cleaned* (optional)

A kuku is a baked omelet somewhat similar to an Italian frittata or an Arab eggah; it is thick and rather fluffy, and stuffed with herbs, vegetables, or meat. It may be eaten hot or cold—it keeps well in the refrigerator for two or three days—as an appetizer, side dish, or light main dish with yogurt or salad and bread. Kukus are traditionally made on the stovetop, but my oven version is much simpler. A fresh herb kuku such as this one is a traditional New Year's dish in Iran. The green herbs symbolize rebirth, and the eggs, fertility and happiness for the year to come.

1. Preheat the oven to 350°F. Pour the oil into an 8-inch baking dish lined with parchment paper.

2. Break the eggs into a large bowl. Add the baking powder, *advieh*, salt, and pepper. Lightly beat in the garlic, chopped herbs, flour, and fenugreek. Adjust seasoning.

3. Pour the egg mixture into the dish and bake uncovered for 45 to 50 minutes, until the edge is golden brown.

4. Serve the *kuku* from the baking dish, or unmold it by loosening the edge with a knife and inverting the dish onto a serving platter. Remove the parchment paper. NUSH-E JAN!

Eggplant Kuku

Kuku-ye bademjan

SERVINGS: *4*
PREP TIME: *30 min.*
COOKING TIME: *45 min.*

2 large or 6 small
  eggplants (about 2
  pounds), peeled and
  cut into thin strips*
1 egg white, lightly
  beaten
½ cup vegetable oil,
  butter, or ghee*
2 large onions, peeled
  and thinly sliced
4 cloves garlic, peeled
  and crushed
4 eggs
4 tablespoons chopped
  fresh parsley
¼ teaspoon ground
  saffron threads,*
  dissolved in 1
  tablespoon hot water
Juice of 1 lime
1 teaspoon baking
  powder
1 tablespoon all-
  purpose flour
1 teaspoon salt
¼ teaspoon freshly
  ground black pepper

1. Peel the eggplants, cut them lengthwise in quarters if they are large, and salt them to remove bitterness if necessary.* Brush each side of the eggplant pieces with egg white to reduce the oil needed for frying.

2. In a skillet, heat 4 tablespoons oil over medium heat. Add the onion and stir-fry for 10 minutes, until translucent.

3. Add the eggplant and garlic and stir-fry 10 minutes longer, until all sides are lightly golden brown. Remove from heat and allow to cool.

4. Preheat the oven to 350°F. Pour 4 tablespoons of oil into an 8-inch baking dish lined with parchment paper.

5. Break the eggs into a large bowl. Add the parsley, saffron water, lime juice, baking powder, flour, salt, and pepper. Beat thoroughly with a fork. Add the eggplant, onion and garlic and mix thoroughly.

6. Pour the mixture into the dish and bake uncovered for 45 to 50 minutes, until the edge is golden brown.

7. Serve the *kuku* from the baking dish or unmold it by loosening the edge with a knife and inverting the dish onto a serving platter. Remove the parchment paper. NUSH-E JAN*!*

Chicken, Meat & Fish

Persian Chicken Salad

Rice-Stuffed Chicken

Sweet & Sour Stuffed Chicken

Chickpea Patties

Rice Meatballs

Fruit & Vegetable Casserole

Pistachio-Stuffed Leg of Lamb

Herb & Tamarind Shrimp

Platonic Fish

Pomegranate Fish

Garlic & Seville Orange Fish

Sweet & Sour Fish

Herb-Stuffed Fish

Grilled Fish with Sumac

Lamb Rib Chops Kabab

Fillet Kabab

Shish Kabab

Chicken Kabab

Lamb Kabab

Ground Beef, Lamb or Chicken Kabab

CHICKEN, MEAT & FISH

One should eat first that which swims, then that which flies, then that which walks on two legs, and last that which walks on four, says a fourth-century Pahlavi text, placing the abundance of creation in the service of man. The writer's list is, of course, for privileged man: Throughout history, the best fish, game, poultry, and meat were prestige foods, usually enjoyed by the ruling classes. Not surprisingly, it was in Persian palace kitchens that the refined layerings of flavor that distinguish Iranian meat and fish cookery were first developed.

Refinement does not necessarily mean elaboration or difficulty. Iranian kababs originated as the food of the soldier, the huntsman, and the herder. They are meat cooked in the most primitive way, over an open fire. That is all the Persian word, kabab, now familiar in variants the world over, means: grilled meat. It is the marination in aromatics, spices, and tart liquids like lime juice, balancing and enhancing the meat's richness and the fire's smoky tang, that gives kababs their complexity.

Combined with another Persian creation, *chelow* (saffron steamed rice, pages 89-90), kababs make Iran's national dish, *chelow-kabab*. It once was served everywhere, from the grandest houses to the humblest street stalls, but the best was made in bazaar cookshops. First came the *chelow*, covered with a tin cloche to keep it warm. Then came the waiter, with as many as ten skewers still smoking from the grill in his left hand and a piece of *lavash* bread in his right. He would hold a skewer over the uncovered rice mound, steady the meat with the bread, and whisk the skewer out with a flourish, leaving the kababs sizzling on the rice. One might have chosen *kabab-e kubideh* (ground beef, lamb or chicken, page 83) *kabab-e barg* (fillet kabab, page 76), or the combination of both called *soltani*, meaning "kingly." It didn't matter: With *lavash* bread, grilled tomatoes, trimmings like fresh herbs, scallions, yogurt sauces, and Persian pickles, any kababs made a royal feast. As you will see, it is one simple to duplicate at home.

Kababs are only one element in the repertoire of Persian meat and fish cookery, however. On the following pages you will find fish and seafood dishes from the Persian Gulf and Caspian provinces. There are hearty country dishes like meatballs, meat patties, and casseroles meant for big appetites. And for festive dinners there are a few dishes from the Persian grand cuisine, such as *Morgh-e tu por ba berenj* (rice-stuffed chicken, page 58) and *Run-e Bareh-ye tu por ba pesteh* (pistachio-stuffed leg of lamb, page 66). These require no unusual techniques to prepare, but the interplay of sweet and tart fruits and nuts with the chicken and meat give an authentic taste of courtly Persia. They are, you might say, *soltani*.

THE ULTIMATE KABAB

Kababs are true convenience cooking: The prudent cook will keep meat marinating in the refrigerator to serve to unexpected guests or hungry husbands and children. At dinner time, while the *chelow* cooks, she can fire the grill and prepare the kababs.

Of course if you have no charcoal grill, you can cook the marinated meat, skewered or not, in a broiler and it will taste good. Really wonderful kababs, however, depend on the subtle blending of flavors and fragrances provided by herbs, garlic, onion, tart agents like lime juice, and the rich, smoky perfume of glowing coals.

The techniques and equipment for achieving such easy perfection derive from centuries of experience. Meat, poultry, fish, or vegetables are prepared as in any of the recipes that follow. For grilling, the ingredients should be cut into relatively thin pieces that permit even cookery, not into thick chunks. The pieces are best threaded on the stainless-steel skewers—available at kitchenware shops and Persian markets—most appropriate to their shapes. For cubed meat, use narrow, ⅛-inch wide skewers; and for meat in strips, use ⅜-inch wide skewers. For ground-meat kababs use flat, 1-inch wide skewers propped on the grill rim or on widely spaced fire bricks to prevent the meat from touching and sticking to the grill surface.

Persian Chicken Salad
Salad-e olivieh

SERVINGS: *6*
PREP TIME: *30 min. plus 15 min. refrigeration*
COOKING TIME: *none*

❧

1 pound skinless boned chicken leg and breast cut into ½-inch strips
1 small onion, peeled and finely chopped
1 teaspoon salt
4 carrots, peeled and chopped
2 cups fresh shelled or frozen green peas
2 scallions, chopped
2 celery stalks, chopped
5 large potatoes, boiled and chopped
3 medium cucumbers fresh or pickled, sliced
½ cup chopped fresh parsley
⅔ cup green or black olives, pitted and chopped
3 hard-boiled eggs, peeled and sliced (optional)

DRESSING
1 cup chicken broth*
3 cups mayonnaise
2 tablespoons Dijon mustard
¼ cup olive oil
¼ cup red wine vinegar
¼ cup fresh lime juice
1½ teaspoons salt
1 teaspoon freshly ground black pepper

1. Place the chicken in a pot along with the onion, salt, and ½ cup water. Bring to a boil, reduce heat to low, cover and simmer for 30 minutes. When the chicken is done, drain it, reserving the broth. Let the chicken cool.

2. Steam the carrots and shelled peas for 5 minutes and set aside. (For frozen peas, follow the package directions.)

3. To make the dressing, thoroughly mix the chicken broth, mayonnaise, mustard, olive oil, vinegar, lime juice, salt, and pepper in a large bowl; or use a blender.

4. Combine the chicken, prepared vegetables, and eggs with the rest of the ingredients. Pour the dressing over the mixture and toss well. Adjust the seasoning to taste.

5. Transfer the salad to a flat plate and chill for at least 15 minutes or up to 24 hours. Serve with *lavash* bread, hot pita bread, or French bread, and any kind of green salad. NUSH-E JAN!

Variation: Instead of combining all the ingredients in Step 4, you may arrange all the ingredients separately on a serving platter and put the dressing in a small bowl on the side as shown.

Rice-Stuffed Chicken

Morgh-e tu por ba berenj

SERVINGS: 4
PREP TIME: *35 min.*
COOKING TIME: *1½ hours*

½ cup long-grain rice
2 small frying chickens
   (about 5 pounds
   total), or 4 Cornish
   game hens
2 teaspoons salt
½ cup vegetable oil,
   butter, or ghee*
2 large onions, peeled
   and thinly sliced
2 cloves garlic, peeled
   and crushed
½ tablespoon Persian
   spice mix (*advieh*)*
1 teaspoon dried rose
   petals
¼ teaspoon freshly
   ground black pepper
1 cup chicken stock or
   water
¼ cup dried barberries,
   cleaned, or ¼ cup
   dried tart cherries*
¼ cup slivered almonds
½ cup raisins
2 tablespoons fresh lime
   juice
¼ teaspoon ground
   saffron threads,*
   dissolved in 1
   tablespoon hot water

When we first moved to America I tried using this traditional Persian rice stuffing with turkey instead of chicken. Ever since, I have delighted Thanksgiving guests by combining the traditional turkey with the unique flavors of a Persian stuffing. The stuffing can be made with wild rice, creating even more of a Persian-American blend. If you use wild rice, check the package for cooking instructions.

1. Pick over and wash the rice once.

2. Wash the chickens in cold water, pat them dry, and rub them with 1 teaspoon salt.

3. In a skillet, heat 3 tablespoons oil over medium heat. Add the onions and garlic and fry for 15 to 20 minutes, stirring occasionally, until golden brown. Add the rice, *advieh*, rose petals, 1 teaspoon salt, and pepper, and stir-fry for 2 minutes.

4. Add the chicken stock, cover, and simmer over low heat for 20 minutes. Preheat oven to 400°F.

5. Add the barberries, almonds, raisins, lime juice, and saffron water. Mix well and remove from heat.

6. Stuff the chickens with the rice mixture and truss them.

7. Place the chickens in a greased ovenproof dish or roasting pan, paint each with 1 tablespoon oil or melted butter and cover loosely with aluminum foil.

8. Place the pan in the oven and roast for 1½ hours.

9. Serve the chicken in the baking dish or on a platter, with bread, raw vegetables, fresh herbs, and salad. NUSH-E JAN!

Variation: **Rice-Stuffed Chicken Breasts**
Lay two large, boneless chicken breast halves flat, skin down, and using the flat of a large knife, press down to flatten as much as possible. Place half the rice mixture on each breast, roll up, and pin closed with bamboo skewers. Place side by side in a greased baking pan, cover, and bake for 45 minutes. Remove the chicken from the oven, cut each breast diagonally in 2-inch pieces and serve with bread, raw vegetables, fresh herbs, and salad.

Sweet & Sour Stuffed Chicken

Morgh-e tu por-e torsh-o-shirin

SERVINGS: *4*
PREP TIME: *35 min.*
COOKING TIME: *1½ hours*

2 small frying chickens
  (about 5 pounds
  total), or 4 Cornish
  game hens
2½ teaspoons salt
4 tablespoons vegetable
  oil, butter, or ghee*
1 large onion, peeled
  and thinly sliced
2 cloves garlic, peeled
  and crushed
1 cup finely chopped
  pitted prunes
1 apple, peeled, cored
  and chopped
1 cup finely chopped
  dried apricots
½ cup raisins
¼ teaspoon freshly
  ground black pepper
1 teaspoon ground
  cinnamon
¼ teaspoon ground
  saffron threads,*
  dissolved in 2
  tablespoons hot water
1 teaspoon sugar

This stuffing is also very good with turkey.

1. Wash the chickens in cold water, pat them dry, and rub them with 1 teaspoon salt.

2. In a skillet, heat 2 tablespoons oil over medium heat. Add the onions and garlic and fry for 15 to 20 minutes, stirring occasionally, until golden brown. Preheat the oven to 400°F.

3. Add the prunes, apple, apricots, raisins, 2 teaspoons salt, pepper, cinnamon, saffron water, and sugar and stir-fry 2 minutes longer.

4. Stuff the chickens with the fruit mixture and truss them.

5. Place the chickens in a greased ovenproof dish or roasting pan, paint each with 1 tablespoon oil or melted butter and cover loosely with aluminum foil.

6. Place the pan in the oven and roast for 1½ hours.

7. Serve from the ovenproof dish or arrange the birds on a serving platter. Serve with saffron steamed rice (*chelow*, pages 89-90), bread, salad and fresh herbs. NUSH-E JAN!

Variation: **Sweet & Sour Stuffed Chicken Breasts**
Lay two large, boneless chicken breast halves flat, skin down, and using the flat of a large knife, press down to flatten as much as possible. Place half the fruit mixture on each breast, roll up, and pin closed with bamboo skewers. Place side by side in a greased baking pan, sprinkle with salt and pepper, paint each breast with 1 tablespoon butter, cover, and bake for 45 minutes. Remove the chicken from the oven, cut each breast diagonally in 2-inch pieces and serve with bread, raw vegetables, fresh herbs, and salad.

Chickpea Patties
Shami-e-ard-e Nokhodchi

SERVINGS: *4*
PREP TIME: *10 min. plus 1 hour's refrigeration*
COOKING TIME: *20 min. plus 20 min. for sauce*

2 medium onions, peeled and chopped

1 teaspoon baking soda, dissolved in ½ cup water

2 cups roasted chickpea flour*

½ teaspoon ground saffron threads, dissolved in 2 tablespoons hot water

2 teaspoons Persian spice mix *(advieh)**

1½ teaspoons salt

½ teaspoon freshly ground black pepper

2 eggs

1 pound ground lamb, beef, or veal

2 cups oil or more, for frying

SWEET & SOUR SAUCE

1 onion, peeled and thinly chopped

3 tablespoons vegetable oil, butter, or ghee*

½ teaspoon ground turmeric

1 teaspoon dried mint

½ cup red wine vinegar

½ cup sugar

GARNISH

Parsley, basil, and mint sprigs

1. In a food processor, purée the onion, then add the baking soda water, chickpea flour, saffron water, *advieh*, salt, pepper, and eggs and mix well.

2. Add the meat and mix for one minute to create a soft paste. Cover and refrigerate for at least 1 hour.

3. Place a bowl of warm water next to your cooking pan. With damp hands, separate the meat paste into lumps the size of walnuts. Flatten each lump between your palms into an oval shape and press a hole in the center with your finger.

4. In a skillet, heat 2 cups oil over medium heat until smoking, then fry the patties on each side for about 5 minutes, until golden brown, adding more oil if necessary. There should be enough oil so that the patties are completely immersed in oil.

5. Arrange the patties on a platter, garnish with parsley, basil, and mint sprigs, and serve with warm *lavash* bread and fresh herbs and vegetables.

6. To make the optional sweet and sour sauce, heat 3 tablespoons oil in a skillet and stir-fry the chopped onion for 10 minutes. Add the turmeric, mint, ½ cup water, vinegar, and sugar and bring to a boil. Before serving, simmer the patties in the sauce for 3 minutes or simply pour the sauce into a bowl and serve it on the side with the patties. Serve hot. NUSH-E JAN!

Variation: Yellow Split Pea* Patties
Follow the above recipe, replacing the chickpea flour and ½ cup baking soda water with 3½ cups cooked and mashed yellow split peas.

Rice Meatballs
Kufteh berenji

SERVINGS: *6*
PREP TIME: *35 min.*
COOKING TIME: *1¼ hours*

½ cup yellow split peas*
1 cup long-grain rice
2 teaspoons salt
2 eggs
2 teaspoons Persian
  spice mix (*advieh*)*
¼ teaspoon freshly
  ground black pepper
3 large onions, 1 peeled
  and grated, and 2
  peeled and thinly sliced
1 pound ground meat
  (lamb, veal, or beef)
2 cups chopped fresh
  parsley or ½ cup dried
1 cup chopped fresh dill
  or ¼ cup dried
½ cup chopped fresh
  summer savory or 2
  tablespoons dried
¼ cup chopped fresh
  tarragon or 1
  tablespoon dried
2 cups chopped fresh
  chives or scallions
2 cloves garlic, peeled
  and crushed
½ cup vegetable oil,
  butter, or ghee*
1 cup tomato juice
2 cups water
2 cups beef broth*
¼ cup fresh lime juice
1 teaspoon ground
  turmeric
¼ teaspoon ground
  saffron threads,*
  dissolved in 1
  tablespoon hot water

1. Pick over the rice and split-peas, and rinse once.

2. In a saucepan, bring 4 cups water and ½ teaspoon salt to a boil. Add the split peas and rice and cook, covered, for 30 minutes over medium heat.

3. Using a fine mesh colander, drain the split peas and rice, reserving the liquid, and set aside.

4. Break the eggs into a mixing bowl, add ½ teaspoon salt, the *advieh*, and the pepper and beat well. Add the grated onion, ground meat, parsley, dill, summer savory, tarragon, chives, split peas, and rice. Knead the mixture thoroughly for about 10 minutes until it reaches the consistency of a smooth paste.

5. In a heavy pot, heat ½ cup oil over medium heat. Add the sliced onions and garlic and fry 15 to 20 minutes, stirring occasionally, until golden brown. Add the tomato juice, water, beef broth, the liquid reserved in Step 3, lime juice, turmeric, 1 teaspoon salt, and saffron water. Bring to a boil.

6. Shape the meat paste into balls the size of lemons. Gently place the meatballs in the boiling pot of broth. Reduce the heat so that the broth simmers, cover partially, and simmer gently for 45 minutes, basting the meatballs occasionally with the broth to prevent them from drying out.

7. Cover and cook for 15 minutes longer.

8. Adjust salt to your taste, place the meatballs in a bowl, and gently pour the pan sauce on top. Serve hot with yogurt and *lavash* bread. NUSH-E JAN!

Variation: Sumac or Unripe Plum Meatballs
Replace the lime juice in Step 5 with 2 tablespoons powdered sumac* or 1 cup unripe plums.*

Variation: Curried Spicy Meatballs
Add 2 tablespoons curry powder and 1 teaspoon powdered red pepper in Step 5. Roll the meatballs in bread crumbs and fry them in ¼ cup oil; then add them to the broth. During the last 10 minutes of cooking, add ½ cup beaten yogurt. Serve hot with bread.

Variation: Fava Bean & Dill Meatballs
Replace all the herbs with 4 cups chopped fresh dill and 1 pound washed, shelled fava beans.* Cook the fava beans with the rice and split-peas for 30 minutes and drain. Add the dill. All other cooking times and proportions of spices are the same.

Fruit & Vegetable Casserole

Tas kabab

SERVINGS: 6
PREP TIME: *15 min.*
COOKING TIME: *1½ hours*

4 tablespoons vegetable oil, butter, or ghee*

4 large onions, peeled and sliced

2 pounds lean filet or shoulder of lamb, veal, or beef, boned and thinly sliced

2 cloves garlic, peeled and crushed

2 quinces, or apples, cored and sliced

1 small eggplant (about ½ pound), peeled and sliced into thin strips*

2 carrots, peeled and sliced

3 tomatoes, peeled and sliced

2 large potatoes, peeled and sliced

1 cup pitted prunes

2 cups dried apricots

1 teaspoon Persian spice mix (*advieh*)*

¼ teaspoon ground turmeric

2 teaspoons salt

¼ teaspoon freshly ground black pepper

1 cup tomato juice

½ teaspoon ground saffron threads, dissolved in 1 tablespoon hot water*

1 tablespoon unripe grape powder*

1 tablespoon dried Persian lime powder* or sumac powder*

The Persian name for this casserole means "kabab in a copper kettle." The careful layering and slow cooking of the many and varied ingredients result in the meat becoming tender, juicy, and very tasty.

1. Preheat oven to 400°F.

2. Pour 2 tablespoons oil into a large ovenproof casserole. Layer the ingredients in the following order: onion, meat, garlic, quince, eggplant, carrots, tomatoes, and potatoes. Top with a layer of prunes and apricots. Pour in the remaining oil. Sprinkle *advieh*, turmeric, salt, and pepper on top. Mix together the tomato juice, saffron water, grape powder, and dried Persian lime powder and pour over the meat and vegetables. Cover and cook in the oven for 1½ hours or until the meat is tender. Season to taste.

3. Serve in the casserole with bread, yogurt, salad, and fresh herbs. NUSH-E JAN!

Variation: This casserole is traditionally cooked in a heavy Dutch oven on the stove over low heat for 2 hours, or until the meat is tender.

Pistachio-Stuffed Leg of Lamb

Run-e Bareh-ye tu por ba pesteh

SERVINGS: *12*
PREP TIME: *45 min.*
COOKING TIME: *1½ hours*

5 to 6 pound butterflied
   leg of lamb
10 cloves garlic, peeled
   and sliced
3 tablespoons vegetable
   oil, butter, or ghee*
2 large onions, peeled
   and thinly sliced
1 cup long-grain white
   rice, washed and
   rinsed
2 tablespoons salt
1 teaspoon freshly
   ground black pepper
1 teaspoon turmeric
½ cup chopped almonds
½ cup chopped unsalted
   pistachios
2 cups raisins
¼ cup chopped apricots
½ cup dried barberries,
   cleaned*
½ cup chopped, pitted
   dates
2 apples, peeled, cored,
   and chopped
½ teaspoon cayenne
   pepper
2 teaspoons ground
   saffron threads,*
   dissolved in ¼ cup hot
   water
Juice of 1 lime
2 tablespoons Persian
   spice mix (*advieh*)*

In Iran this spectacular dish is prepared with a whole baby lamb and is served on festive occasions, often as the centerpiece of a lavish wedding feast. Several lambs would be prepared well ahead of time to serve all the guests, as whole lambs take about 5 to 6 hours to cook completely on a spit.

1. Rinse the lamb and pat dry.

2. Using the point of a small knife, make 10 incisions in the lamb. Insert a sliced garlic clove in each incision.

3. In a large skillet, heat the oil over medium heat. Add the onions and fry for 15 to 20 minutes, stirring occasionally, until golden brown. Add the rice and stir-fry 5 minutes longer.

4. Add 2 cups water, the salt, pepper, turmeric, almonds, pistachios, raisins, apricots, barberries, dates, apples, cayenne pepper, saffron water, lime juice, and *advieh* and bring to a boil. Reduce the heat to low, cover and simmer for 20 minutes.

5. Preheat oven to 400°F. Lay the stuffing on the lamb and sew shut using a large trussing needle and strong kitchen twine. Place the lamb in a large, heavy ovenproof baking dish.

6. In a saucepan, mix 2 tablespoons melted butter, 1 teaspoon salt, 1 teaspoon freshly ground black pepper, ¼ teaspoon ground saffron threads* dissolved in 2 tablespoons hot water, and ½ cup fresh lime juice. Set this mixture aside.

7. Cover the lamb with aluminum foil and bake for 1 hour.

8. Uncover the lamb and bake 30 minutes longer, basting occasionally with the mixture from Step 6. The lamb will be rare (pink on the inside) when a meat thermometer inserted in the thickest part registers 150°F; for well done lamb, the temperature will be 160°F to 165°F.

9. Lay the lamb on a serving platter and serve with fresh herbs and vegetables. NUSH-E JAN!

Herb & Tamarind Shrimp

Ghaliyeh maygu

SERVINGS: *4*
PREP TIME: *25 min.*
COOKING TIME: *40 min.*

✣

4 tablespoons vegetable oil, butter, or ghee*
1 large onion, peeled and thinly sliced
10 cloves garlic, peeled and crushed
3 cups chopped fresh coriander leaves (cilantro)
2 large tomatoes, peeled* and crushed
1 cup chopped fresh fenugreek or 3 tablespoons dried
¼ cup chopped fresh basil
2 teaspoons curry powder
½ teaspoon freshly ground black pepper
½ teaspoon ground cayenne pepper
⅔ cup tamarind paste* diluted in ½ cup water
1 pound raw shrimp, peeled, deveined, and patted dry

This recipe comes from the Persian Gulf.

1. In a skillet, heat 2 tablespoons oil over medium heat. Add the onion and garlic and stir-fry for 10 minutes, until translucent. Add the coriander and stir-fry 3 minutes longer, then add the tomato and stir-fry 5 more minutes.

2. Add the fenugreek, basil, curry powder, black pepper, cayenne pepper, and tamarind liquid. Mix well, cover, and simmer over low heat for 20 minutes. Adjust seasoning and set aside.

3. Just prior to serving, in a skillet, heat 2 tablespoons oil over medium heat. Stir-fry the shrimp for 2 to 3 minutes, just until it changes color. Be careful not to overcook—shrimp loses its tenderness when overcooked. Add to the sauce.

4. Add salt to taste and adjust seasoning. Serve with saffron steamed rice (*chelow*, pages 89-90). NUSH-E JAN!

Variation: Replace the shrimp with scallops, mackerel or grouper fillets.

Platonic Fish
Mahi-ye aflatuni

SERVINGS: *4*
PREP TIME: *20 min.*
COOKING TIME: *15 min.*

4 tablespoons vegetable oil, butter, or ghee*
1 cup washed and chopped scallions
2 cloves garlic, peeled and crushed
1 cup pomegranate juice or 1 tablespoon pomegranate paste dissolved in ½ cup water*
½ cup unripe grape juice or 1 teaspoon powdered unripe grape*
1 cup Seville orange juice* or a mixture of 4 tablespoons fresh lime juice and ½ cup fresh orange juice
1 cup tomato juice
1 teaspoon salt
½ teaspoon Persian spice mix (*advieh*)*
1 tablespoon sugar or honey
4 fish fillets, ½-inch to ¼-inch thick (sea bass, trout, orange roughy, or rockfish, about 2 pounds)
1 tablespoon flour
½ cup pomegranate seeds* for garnish (optional)

This recipe is from the Gilan region in Northern Iran near the Caspian Sea. In Persian, the word aflatuni *means "platonic," but why this recipe is called that is unknown. Persian-Greek relations, of course, go back a long ways. The Greek historian Herodotus, wrote more than 2500 years ago: "The first thing the Ionians and Aeolians did after the Lydians had been defeated by the Persians was send a delegation to Cyrus at Sardis, since they wanted the terms of their subjection to him to be the same as they had been with Croesus. Cyrus listened to the delegation's suggestions and then told them a story. A pipe-player once saw some fish in the sea, he said, and played his pipes in the hope that they would come out on to the shore. His hopes came to nothing, so he grabbed a net, cast it over a large number of the fish, and hauled them in. When he saw the fish flopping about, he said to them, 'It's no good dancing now, because you weren't willing to come out dancing when I played my pipes.' The reason Cyrus told this story to the Ionians and Aeolians was that the Ionians had in fact refused to listen to Cyrus earlier, when he had sent a message asking them to rise up against Croesus, whereas now that the war was over and won, they were ready to do what he wanted."*

1. In a saucepan, heat 1 tablespoon of the oil over medium heat. Add the scallions and garlic and stir-fry for 1 minute. Add the pomegranate juice, unripe grape juice, Seville orange juice, tomato juice, ½ teaspoon salt, *advieh*, and sugar. Bring to a boil and remove from heat. Taste the sauce: It should be sweet and sour. If necessary, add more sugar.

2. Wash the fish and pat it dry. Sprinkle with ½ teaspoon salt and 1 tablespoon flour.

3. In a skillet, heat the remaining 3 tablespoons oil over medium heat. Sauté the fish for 2 minutes on each side.

4. Pour the sauce over the fish, cover, and simmer over low heat for 5 to 10 minutes. Remove from the heat, garnish with a few pomegranate seeds, and serve with saffron steamed rice (*chelow*, pages 89-90). NUSH-E JAN!

Pomegranate Fish

Mahi-ye tu por ba anar

SERVINGS: *4*
PREP TIME: *15 min.*
COOKING TIME: *30 min.*

1 large firm-fleshed
white fish such as
John Dory, sea bass,
or halibut (about 2
pounds), or 4 fillets of
rockfish, orange
roughy or salmon, ¼-
inch thick
1 teaspoon salt
4 tablespoons vegetable
oil, butter, or ghee*
1 onion, peeled and
thinly sliced
3 cloves garlic, peeled
and crushed
¼ teaspoon freshly
ground black pepper
¼ cup chopped walnuts
1 teaspoon angelica
powder*
1 tablespoon candied
orange peel*
1 cup pomegranate juice
or 3 tablespoons
pomegranate paste*
diluted in ⅓ cup water
1 tablespoon sugar or
honey
½ teaspoon ground
saffron threads,*
dissolved in 2
tablespoons hot water
2 tablespoons fresh lime
juice
3 tablespoons
pomegranate seeds*
for garnish

1. Wash the fish, pat it dry, and rub both sides with the salt. Preheat the oven to 400°F.

2. In a skillet, heat 2 tablespoons oil over medium heat. Add the onion and garlic and fry for 10 to 15 minutes, stirring occasionally, until golden brown. Add the pepper, walnuts, angelica powder, candied orange peel, pomegranate juice, and sugar; stir-fry for 3 minutes and remove from the heat.

3. Place the fish in a greased baking dish, stuff the fish with the mixture from Step 2, and pin the cavity shut using skewers. Or, if using fillets, place a quarter of the fruit mixture on each fillet, roll the fillet up, and pin it shut with skewers. Pour the saffron water and lime juice over the fish and dot the fish with 2 tablespoons oil.

4. Place the fish in the oven and bake for 10 to 15 minutes, until the fish flakes easily with a fork, basting from time to time.

5. Arrange the fish on a serving platter. Pour the sauce from the baking dish over the fish, and sprinkle with the pomegranate seeds.

6. Serve with saffron steamed rice (*chelow*, pages 89-90). NUSH-E JAN!

Garlic & Seville Orange Fish

Mahi-ye sir-dagh ba narenj

SERVINGS: *4*
PREP TIME: *10 min.*
COOKING TIME: *20 min.*

4 fillets of red snapper,
  orange roughy,
  rockfish, or sea bass
  (¼-inch to ½-inch
  thick , about 2 pounds)
2 tablespoons all-
  purpose flour
2 teaspoons salt
4 tablespoons vegetable
  oil, butter, or ghee*
10 cloves garlic, peeled
½ teaspoon ground
  turmeric or saffron
  threads*
1 teaspoon freshly
  ground black pepper
½ cup fish broth or
  water
1 cup Seville orange
  juice or a mixture of
  ½ cup fresh squeezed
  orange juice and ¼
  cup lime juice*

1. Wash the fish, pat dry, and dust both sides with 1 tablespoon of the flour and 1 teaspoon salt.

2. In a large skillet, heat 2 tablespoons oil over medium heat. Add the fish and sauté each side for 2 minutes. Remove it from skillet and set aside.

3. In the same skillet, heat 2 tablespoons oil over medium heat. Add the garlic and stir-fry for 5 minutes, until golden brown.

4. Add the turmeric, 1 teaspoon salt, and the pepper, and stir-fry 1 minute longer. Add the fish broth.

5. Dissolve 1 tablespoon flour in the Seville orange juice and add to the skillet. Bring to a boil, remove from heat, and season to taste.

6. Just prior to serving, return the fish to the skillet and simmer for 2 minutes, until the fish is tender.

7. Remove the pan from heat; place the fish on a serving platter and garnish with fresh herbs and scallions. Pour the sauce over it and serve with saffron steamed rice (*chelow*, pages 89-90) and fresh herbs. NUSH-E JAN!

Sweet & Sour Fish
Mahi-ye tu por-e torsh-o shirin

SERVINGS: 4
PREP TIME: *15 min.*
COOKING TIME: *30 min.*

1 large fish (sea bass, salmon, rockfish), cleaned and scaled, or 4 thick fillets of sea bass, flounder, or orange roughy (¼-inch to ½-inch , about 2 pounds)

2 teaspoons salt

4 tablespoons vegetable oil, butter or ghee*

½ cup finely chopped scallions

2 cloves garlic, peeled and crushed

¼ cup chopped, pitted dates

¼ cup finely chopped dried apricots

⅓ cup slivered unsalted pistachios

⅓ cup slivered blanched almonds

1 tablespoon candied orange peel*

Juice of 3 limes or lemons

½ teaspoon ground cinnamon

¼ teaspoon freshly ground black pepper

¼ teaspoon ground saffron threads,* dissolved in 2 tablespoons hot water

2 tablespoons toasted slivered almonds and unsalted pistachios for garnish

1. Wash the fish, pat dry and rub both sides with 1 teaspoon salt. Preheat the oven to 400°F.

2. In a skillet, heat 2 tablespoons oil over medium heat. Add the scallions and garlic and stir-fry for 10 minutes. Add the dates, apricots, pistachios, almonds, candied orange peel, juice of 1 lime, cinnamon, 1 teaspoon of the salt, pepper, and stir-fry 1 minute longer.

3. Stuff the fish with the mixture from Step 2 and skewer the cavity shut. Or, if using fillets, place a quarter of the fruit mixture on each fillet, roll the fillet up, and skewer shut. Lay the fish in a greased baking dish. Pour the saffron water and the rest of the oil and lime juice over the fish.

4. Place in the preheated oven and bake for 15 to 20 minutes, basting from time to time with the pan juices, until the fish flakes easily with a fork.

5. Arrange the fish on a serving platter or serve from the baking dish. Sprinkle with toasted slivered almonds and pistachios and pour the juices from the baking dish over the fish.

6. Serve with saffron steamed rice (*chelow*, pages 89-90) and fresh herbs. NUSH-E JAN!

Note: An alternative way to cook the fillets is to place the stuffing in the center of a greased baking dish. Cover it with the fish, pour the saffron water, oil, and juice over the fish, and bake as directed.

Herb-Stuffed Fish
Mahi-ye tu por ba sabzi

SERVINGS: *4*
PREP TIME: *30 min.*
COOKING TIME: *20–30 min.*

1 large fish (sea bass, salmon, rockfish), cleaned and scaled, or 4 fillets of sea bass, flounder, or orange roughy (¼-inch to ½-inch thick, about 2 pounds)

2 teaspoons salt

3 tablespoons vegetable oil, butter, or ghee*

2 cloves garlic, peeled and crushed

½ cup chopped fresh parsley

2 tablespoons chopped fresh tarragon

4 scallions, chopped

1 tablespoon chopped fresh coriander (cilantro)

¼ cup chopped fresh mint or 2 tablespoons dried

1 cup finely ground walnuts

¼ cup dried barberries, cleaned*

¼ cup raisins

¼ cup fresh lime juice

¼ teaspoon freshly ground black pepper

½ teaspoon ground saffron threads,* dissolved in 2 tablespoons hot water

1 lime or 2 Seville oranges,* cut in half for garnish

1. Wash the fish, pat dry and rub both sides with 1 teaspoon salt. Preheat oven to 400°F.

2. In a skillet, heat 2 tablespoons oil over medium heat. Add the garlic, parsley, tarragon, scallions, coriander, and mint and stir-fry for 10 minutes. Add the walnuts, barberries, raisins, lime juice, 1 teaspoon of the salt, and pepper; mix well and remove from heat.

3. Fill the fish with the herb stuffing and skewer the cavity shut. Or, if using fillets, place a quarter of the herb mixture on each fillet, roll the fillet up, and skewer shut. Lay the fish in a greased baking dish. Sprinkle the fish with the remaining oil and saffron water and place in the oven. Bake for 20 to 30 minutes, until the fish flakes easily with a fork. Baste occasionally with pan juices.

4. Arrange the fish on a serving platter and garnish with lime or Seville orange halves.

5. Serve with saffron steamed rice (*chelow*, pages 89-90) and fresh herbs. *NUSH-E JAN!*

Note: An alternative way to cook the fillets is to place the stuffing in the center of a greased baking dish. Cover it with the fish, pour the saffron water, oil, and juice over the fish, and bake as directed.

Grilled Fish with Sumac
Kabab-e mahi ba somaq

SERVINGS: *4*

PREP TIME: *10 min. plus 30 min. marination*

COOKING TIME: *6–10 min.*

1 large or 4 small firm-fleshed white fish fillets such as John Dory, red snapper, sea bass, salmon, rockfish, swordfish (about 2 pounds)

2 cloves garlic, peeled and crushed

1 teaspoon salt

½ teaspoon freshly ground black pepper

½ cup fresh lime juice

½ cup sumac powder*

2 tablespoons vegetable oil, butter, or ghee*

1. Wash the fillets, pat dry and rub both sides with garlic, salt and pepper.

2. Place the fillets in a baking dish and squeeze lime juice over them. Sprinkle both sides with sumac powder to completely cover. Cover and refrigerate for 30 minutes or up to 8 hours.

3. Just prior to serving, preheat the oven to 500°F. Uncover the fish and pour 2 tablespoons of oil over it. Bake in the upper level of the oven for 6 to 10 minutes until crispy and brown. Alternatively, you can grill the fish over hot coals for approximately 3-5 minutes on each side.

4. Serve with saffron steamed rice (*chelow*, pages 89-90). NUSH-E JAN!

Lamb Rib Chops Kabab
Sishlik

SERVINGS: *4*
PREP TIME: *20 min. plus 8 hours marination*
COOKING TIME: *10 min.*

24 small, single lamb rib chops (French cut)

FOR MARINADE
1 large onion, thinly sliced
1 bulb garlic (10-12 cloves) peeled and crushed
2 tablespoons slivered orange peel with bitterness removed*
1 cup fresh lime juice
2 teaspoons salt
1 teaspoon freshly ground black pepper
2 tablespoons olive oil
1 cup plain yogurt
½ teaspoon ground saffron threads,* dissolved in 2 tablespoon hot water

FOR BASTING
2 tablespoons melted butter
Juice of 2 limes
½ teaspoon freshly ground black pepper
½ teaspoon coarse salt

FOR COOKING & GARNISH
6 thin metal or bamboo skewers soaked in water for 2 hours
1 package (12-ounces) of *lavash* bread
Bunch of fresh scallions
Bunch of fresh basil

1. Rinse the lamb rib chops in a colander with cool water and pat dry thoroughly with a paper towel. Prepare the marinade in a large, deep pyrex dish mixing the onion, garlic, slivered orange peel, lime juice, salt, pepper, olive oil, yogurt and saffron water. Rub the rib chops thoroughly on both sides in the marinade inside the dish, one at a time. Cover and marinate for at least 8 hours in the refrigerator. Turn the chops once during this time.

2. Start a bed of charcoal at least 30 minutes before you want to cook and let it burn until the coals glow. You can use a hair dryer to accelerate this process.

3. Meanwhile, thread the chops flat side up onto flat skewers; the skewers will go through the bone, which is soft.

4. For basting, combine the butter, lime juice, salt, and pepper in a small saucepan. Keep warm over very low heat.

5. When the coals are glowing, place the skewers on the grill. Grill for 2 to 3 minutes on each side, turning occasionally. The total cooking time should be 4 to 6 minutes. The chops should be seared on the outside and juicy on the inside. Baste the chops just before removing from the flame.

6. Spread *lavash* bread on a serving platter. When the chops are done baste both sides again, then steady them with a piece of *lavash* bread while you pull the skewers out. Sprinkle with a little coarse salt. Garnish and cover with *lavash* bread to keep warm, and serve immediately. NUSH-E JAN!

Fillet Kabab

Kabab-e barg

SERVINGS: *4*
PREP TIME: *20 min. plus ½–48 hours marination*
COOKING TIME: *10 min.*

- 2 pounds boned lean loin or sirloin (beef or veal)
- 8 cherry tomatoes, or 4 large tomatoes halved

FOR MARINADE

- Juice of 2 large onions*
- 1 teaspoon freshly ground black pepper
- 2 tablespoons fresh lime juice
- 2 teaspoons salt
- 2 tablespoons olive oil
- 2 tablespoons plain yogurt
- ¼ teaspoon ground saffron threads,* dissolved in 1 tablespoon hot water (optional)

FOR BASTING

- 2 tablespoons melted butter
- Juice of 2 limes
- ½ teaspoon salt
- 1 teaspoon freshly ground black pepper

FOR COOKING & GARNISH

- 6 flat ⅜-inch-wide skewers
- 1 package (12-ounce) of *lavash* bread
- 2 tablespoons sumac powder* (optional)
- Bunch of fresh scallions
- Bunch of fresh basil

1. Cut the meat lengthwise into 3-by-4-by-¼-inch pieces and place it in a large glass or Pyrex dish.

2. Add the onion juice, pepper, lime juice, salt, olive oil, yogurt, and saffron water to the meat and mix well. Cover the meat and marinate for at least 30 minutes, or up to 48 hours in refrigerator. Turn the meat in the marinade twice during this period.

3. Start a bed of charcoal at least 30 minutes before you want to cook and let it burn until the coals glow. You can use a hair dryer to accelerate this process.

4. Meanwhile, thread each piece of meat onto a flat, sword-like skewer, leaving a few inches free on both ends. Pound the meat with the edge of another skewer to tenderize it. Spear the tomatoes on separate skewers.

5. For basting, combine the butter, lime juice, salt, and pepper in a small saucepan. Keep warm over very low heat.

6. When the coals are glowing, brush the tomatoes and meat lightly with the basting mixture. Place the tomatoes on the grill; then 1 minute later place the skewered meat on the grill. Cook 3 to 4 minutes on each side, turning the skewers frequently. The total cooking time should be 6 to 8 minutes. The meat should be seared on the outside, pink and juicy on the inside.

7. Spread *lavash* bread on a serving platter. When the meat is done, steady it firmly with a piece of *lavash* bread while you pull the skewer out. Brush the meat with the basting mixture, and sprinkle with sumac powder to taste. Garnish with grilled tomatoes and cover with *lavash* bread to keep warm.

8. Serve with saffron steamed rice (*chelow*, pages 89-90), *lavash* bread, fresh scallions, and basil or radishes and onions as shown here. *NUSH-E JAN!*

Shish Kabab

Shish Kabab

SERVINGS: *6*
PREP TIME: *30 min. plus 8–24 hours marination*
COOKING TIME: *10 min.*

2 pounds lamb, veal, or beef, from the boned loin or leg, or boneless chicken breast, cut into 2-inch cubes

4 green peppers, seeds and ribs removed, cut into 1-inch squares

6 large tomatoes, quartered

10 cloves garlic, peeled

10 pearl onions or 3 large ones peeled and cut into 2-inch cubes

10 white button mushrooms

10 bay leaves

FOR MARINADE

1 large onion, peeled and sliced

1 cup red wine vinegar

½ cup olive oil

1 teaspoon freshly ground black pepper

1 tablespoon salt

1 cup chopped fresh oregano or 1 teaspoon dried

FOR COOKING & GARNISH

6 bamboo skewers soaked in water for 2 hours

1 cup plain yogurt

1 package (12-ounce) of *lavash* bread

Bunch of fresh scallions

Bunch of fresh basil

1. In a long, shallow glass or Pyrex dish combine all the marinade ingredients and set aside.

2. Thread each piece of meat onto the bamboo skewers, alternating them with pieces of pepper, tomato, garlic, onions, mushrooms, and bay leaves. Place the skewers in the marinade.

3. Agitate the dish so that the marinade coats all sides of the kababs. Cover and marinate for at least 8 hours in the refrigerator. Turn the kababs at least twice, so that each side is equally marinated.

4. Start a bed of charcoal at least 30 minutes before you want to cook and let it burn until the coals glow. You can use a hair dryer to accelerate this process.

5. When the coals are glowing, place the skewers on the grill. Cook for 3 to 5 minutes on each side, turning frequently and basting with the remaining marinade. The total cooking time should be 6 to 10 minutes.

6. Arrange the skewers on a serving platter and serve immediately with *lavash* bread, yogurt, and fresh scallions and fresh herbs. NUSH-E JAN!

Chicken Kabab
Jujeh kabab

SERVINGS: 6
PREP TIME: *20 min. plus
6 hours marination*
COOKING TIME: *15 min.*

2 broiling chickens
  (about 4 pounds
  total), each cut into 10
  pieces, or 4 pounds of
  chicken drumettes, or
  3 pounds boneless
  chicken cut into 1½-
  inch pieces (chicken
  drumettes are tastier
  and cheaper)
10 cherry tomatoes or 4
  large tomatoes, cut
  into quarters
6 flat ⅜-inch wide skewers
2 flat ½-inch wide skewers
2 packages (12-ounces
  each) of *lavash* bread

FOR MARINADE
1 teaspoon ground
  saffron threads,*
  dissolved in 2
  tablespoons hot water
1 cup fresh lime juice
2 tablespoons olive oil
2 large onions, peeled
  and thinly sliced
2 tablespoons plain
  yogurt
2 teaspoons salt
2 teaspoons freshly
  ground black pepper

FOR BASTING
Juice of 1 lime
2 tablespoons butter
½ teaspoon salt
½ teaspoon freshly
  ground black pepper

1. In a large glass or Pyrex bowl with cover, combine 1 teaspoon saffron water, the lime juice, olive oil, onions, yogurt, and salt and pepper. Beat well with a fork. Add the pieces of chicken and toss well. Cover and marinate for at least 6 or up to 48 hours in the refrigerator. Turn the chicken twice during this time.

2. Start a bed of charcoal at least 30 minutes before you want to cook and let it burn until the coals glow. You can use a hair dryer to accelerate this process.

3. Spear the chicken wings, breasts, and legs on different ⅜-inch skewers: They require different cooking times. Spear the tomatoes on the ½-inch skewers.

4. In small saucepan melt the butter and add the remaining saffron water, lime juice, salt, and pepper. Mix well and keep warm over very low heat.

5. When the coals are glowing, grill the chicken and tomatoes for 8 to 15 minutes turning occasionally (drumettes need less time to cook), putting the legs on first, then the breasts and wings. The chicken is done when the juice that runs out is clear rather than pink.

6. Spread *lavash* bread on a serving platter. When the chicken is done, steady it with a piece of *lavash* bread while you pull the skewer out. Brush the chicken with the basting mixture, garnish with halved limes and sprigs of parsley and cover with *lavash* bread to keep warm.

7. Serve immediately with fresh scallions, basil and radishes. NUSH-E JAN!

Note: The kabab I am pulling off the skewer on the facing page is a ground beef kabab (page 83) while the chicken drumettes from this recipe are on the skewer in the middle and to their left is a skewer of lamb kabab (page 82).

Lamb Kabab
Chenjeh kabab

SERVINGS: *4*
PREP TIME: *20 min. plus 24–72 hours marination*
COOKING TIME: *10 min.*

❧

1 pound lean lamb
 tenderloin or leg
 meat, boned and cut
 into 2-inch cubes
4 large tomatoes, halved

FOR MARINADE
1 large onion, peeled
 and sliced
4 cloves garlic, peeled
 and crushed
1 teaspoon salt
½ teaspoon freshly
 ground black pepper
½ cup fresh lime juice
¼ teaspoon ground
 saffron threads,*
 dissolved in 2
 tablespoons hot water

FOR BASTING
½ cup melted butter or
 ghee
2 tablespoons fresh lime
 juice
¼ teaspoon ground
 saffron threads,*
 dissolved in 2
 tablespoons hot water
½ teaspoon salt
½ teaspoon freshly
 ground black pepper

FOR COOKING & GARNISH
6 flat, ⅛-inch-wide
 swordlike skewers
1 package (12 ounces) of
 lavash bread

Traditionally, pieces of sheep tail-fat are threaded between the pieces of the meat to add flavor and keep the meat moist. You can substitute pieces of smoked bacon cut into 2-inch pieces for a similar effect.

1. Pound the lamb pieces lightly with a heavy-bladed knife to tenderize, and make shallow incisions in them. Place the lamb in a large glass or Pyrex bowl.

2. Add the onion, garlic, salt, pepper, lime juice, and saffron water and mix well. Cover and marinate for at least 24 and up to 72 hours in the refrigerator. Turn the meat twice during this time.

3. Start a bed of charcoal at least 30 minutes before you want to cook and let it burn until the coals glow. You can use a hair dryer to accelerate this process.

4. Meanwhile, thread 5 or 6 pieces of meat onto each skewer, leaving a few inches free on both ends. Spear tomatoes onto separate skewers.

5. For basting, combine the butter, lime juice, saffron water, salt, and pepper in a small saucepan. Keep warm over very low heat.

6. When the coals are glowing, place the tomatoes on the grill; then 1 minute later place the skewered meat on the grill. Grill for 3 to 4 minutes on each side, turning frequently, and basting occasionally. The total cooking time should be 6 to 10 minutes. The meat should be seared on the outside, pink and juicy on the inside.

7. Spread *lavash* bread on a serving platter. When the meat is done, steady it with a piece of *lavash* bread while you pull it off the skewer. Brush with the basting mixture, garnish with grilled tomatoes, and cover with *lavash* bread to keep the food warm.

8. Serve immediately with saffron steamed rice (*chelow*, pages 89-90), *lavash* bread, and fresh scallions and basil. NUSH-E JAN!

Ground Beef, Lamb or Chicken Kabab
Kabab-e kubideh

SERVINGS: *6*
PREP TIME: *40 min.*
COOKING TIME: *10 min.*

FOR GROUND MEAT
1 large onion, peeled
1 clove garlic, peeled
2 pounds lean twice-
   ground beef, or 1
   pound each twice-
   ground sirloin and
   lamb shoulder
2 teaspoons salt
1 teaspoon freshly
   ground black pepper
1 tablespoon fresh lime
   juice
½ teaspoon baking soda

FOR GROUND CHICKEN
1 small onion, peeled
5 cloves garlic, peeled
2 pounds ground
   boneless lean chicken
   breast
1 teaspoon salt
½ teaspoon freshly
   ground black pepper
¼ cup olive oil

FOR BASTING
2 tablespoons melted
   butter
½ teaspoon fresh lime
   juice
¼ teaspoon salt

FOR COOKING & GARNISH
12 flat 1-inch skewers
1 package (12 ounces) of
   lavash bread
½ cup sumac powder*
   or 2 limes, halved

1. Just prior to preparing kababs, purée the onion and garlic in a food processor and set aside.

2. In a large, warmed skillet, combine the meat or chicken with the other kabab ingredients, gradually adding the puréed onion and garlic. Knead with your hands for 5 to 15 minutes to form a paste that will adhere well to cooking skewers. Cover the paste and let stand for 15 minutes at room temperature.

3. With damp hands, divide the meat paste equally into 12 lumps. Roll each into a sausage shape 5 inches long and mold it firmly around a flat, sword-like skewer. Cover and keep in a cool place.

4. Start a bed of charcoal at least 30 minutes before you want to cook and let it burn until the coals glow. You can use a hair dryer to accelerate this process.

5. For basting, combine the butter, lime juice, and salt in a small saucepan. Keep warm over very low heat.

6. When the coals are glowing, gently arrange the skewers on the grill 3 inches above the coals (fire bricks make good platforms for the skewers), keeping in mind that the ground meat should not touch the grill. Let the kababs cook a few seconds, just until they change color; then turn the skewers gently to color the other side of the meat. This keeps the meat from falling apart. Then turn gently once more to brown each side.

7. Grill the meat 3 to 5 minutes on each side, and brush it with basting mixture just before removing it from the grill. The total cooking time should be 6 to 10 minutes. The meat should be seared on the outside, pink and juicy on the inside. If this kabab is overcooked it will become very rubbery, like a sausage.

8. Spread *lavash* bread on a serving platter. First loosen the meat from the ends of the skewers with a knife. Then, using a piece of *lavash* bread, hold down the meat and very gently slide it off the skewers. Arrange the meat on the bread, sprinkle with sumac or lime juice to taste, and cover with more *lavash* bread to keep warm.

9. Serve immediately with saffron steamed rice (*chelow*, pages 89-90) or bread, fresh scallions, basil, and yogurt. NUSH-E JAN!

Rice

Saffron Steamed Plain Rice

Plain Rice: Cooker Method

Smothered Rice

Jeweled Rice

Rice with Tomato

Rice with Tomato: Cooker Method

Rice with Lentils & Dates

Rice with Green Beans & Tomatoes

Rice with Noodles & Dates

Rice with Cabbage & Cumin

Rice with Apricots

Dill Rice with Fava Beans

Sweet Rice with Orange Peel

Rice with Tart Cherries

Barberry Rice

Golden Crusted Saffron Rice Mold

ℛICE

Darius the Great, some say, introduced rice growing to likely regions of his vast empire in the sixth century BCE. A plant of tropic and subtropic Asia, it flourished in the similar climate of the provinces around the Caspian Sea and eventually became the staff of life for that region, as bread was for the rest of Iran.

When rice is a staple like this—a stomach filler, a vehicle for other foods—it is generally cooked quite simply by steaming. But over the centuries, in Iran as in Asia, rice cultivation became increasingly sophisticated and the grain itself a luxury. Not all rice is luxurious of course. Iran grew (and grows) ordinary rices like *champa*, first developed along the coast of Vietnam. *Champa* is a coarse, low-gluten grain with the great virtue that it flourishes in poor soil and is tough and drought resistant. But there are rarer, long-grained, fragrant rices and Iran grows some of the finest in the world. They include *dom-siah*, black-tailed rice; *darbari*, imperial court; *ambar-bu*, amber scented; *khanjari*, dagger shaped; and *shikari*, sweet.

These are the sorts of rices esteemed in princely courts and turned by royal cooks into splendid dishes that are the crowns of Iranian cuisine. Judging by surviving Persian cookbooks, written for the Safavid court, the age of invention was the sixteenth century. It was then that the elaborate rice cookery unique to Iran appeared; and while people no longer eat some of the more startling Safavid creations, such as rice dyed blue with indigo or studded with real jewels, the techniques of the Safavids still produce matchless dishes of golden grain, fragrant with spices, herbs, fruits, or meats and rich with clarified butter.

Creating such a dish is easier than it might seem. It requires first of all the proper rice. Iranian rices are not available in the US, but Indian basmati rice, which is like the Persian varieties and gives off much the same flowery scent during cooking, is sold in many supermarkets. Or you can buy it at any of the Persian or Indian specialty grocery stores. I recommend the variety known as *Lal Quilla,* which can be hard to find, or *Pari* which is more readily available. They are sold in 4½-pound plastic bags, and 10-pound sacks, but for convenience I buy it in 40-pound sacks, mix it with a pound of salt to repel insects and mold; and store it in a big popcorn tin with a cover.

You may also use American long-grain rice for Iranian cooking, as explained in the recipes in this section. The results will be good, but the dishes will lack the sublime fragrance and taste that finer rices provide. Never use "converted" rice, which is without texture and flavor. As you will see in the master recipes that begin this section, basmati rice requires preliminary preparation. You must pick over the rice to remove grit, then wash it gently, as described, in five changes of warm water: When the washed rice is cooked, it gives off a delicate aroma that unwashed rice can never have. Cooks around the Caspian also soak their rice in salted water, allowing 8 cups of water and 2 tablespoons of salt per pound of rice. They believe this firms the rice and keeps the grains separate and fluffy during cooking. I have found that basmati rice cooks to perfection without soaking.

Once the rice is washed, it can be used in any of three ways. The simplest is *kateh,* a traditional Caspian dish (page 92). To make it, rice, water, and salt are cooked uncovered until the water is absorbed; then butter is added, the pot is covered, and the rice is steamed. It emerges as a compact cake with a crusty surface. In the Caspian provinces, this rice is eaten hot with milk and jam or cold with cheese and garlic for breakfast; it provides a cushion for meat, fowl, fish, or *khoresh* for lunch or dinner.

For the more fragrant *chelow* (pages 89-90), the washed rice is boiled, drained, and rinsed. Then some of it is mixed with oil or butter, yogurt, and seasonings, and spread over the bottom of the rice pot to form a base crust; the rest of the rice is heaped on top, and the whole is steamed. The result is a mound of tender, fluffy, rice grains with a rich golden—never dark brown or scorched—crust called *tah dig* (from the Persian for "bottom of the pot"). Its quality is the mark of an Iranian cook's talent. *Chelow* is eaten with khoresh (*chelow-khoresh*), or with kababs (*chelow kabab*), the Iranian national dish.

The third famous rice style is *polow* (recipes pages 93-112), essentially a variant of *chelow*. For *polow*, the cooked rice is layered with meat and seasonings and fruits or vegetables, then steamed. Again the *tah dig* forms, but now it is enriched not only with butter but with the complex flavors of meat and fruit juices, aromatics, and spices. With appetizers and dessert, *polow* makes a memorable meal.

THE ALL-IMPORTANT RICE POT

To make perfect Persian rice, with grains that are firm but tender and a golden *tah dig* that lifts smoothly out, you will need a deep pot with a nonstick surface and a tight lid. For convenience and perfection every time, however, I recommend a rice cooker, a wonderful invention: The cooking process is simpler, the cooker's nonstick surface ensures a good *tah dig*, and because its temperature does not vary, the rice is consistently excellent. In addition, most rice cookers stop automatically when the rice is done and keep it warm for hours without drying or burning.

Department stores, kitchenware stores, Persian markets, and catalogs all stock rice cookers ranging in capacity from 5 to 10 cups and in price from $20 to $200. The model I have used for the last 20 years is the National Deluxe, which costs about $100 and is perfect for Persian cooking.

Instructions for using a rice cooker in this section (pages 90 and 95) refer to the National Deluxe. If you have a different model, be sure to check the instructions and adjust measurements and cooking times accordingly.

Saffron Steamed Plain Basmati Rice

Chelow

SERVINGS: *6*
PREP TIME: *5 min.*
COOKING TIME: *1¼ hours*

3 cups long-grain white basmati rice
8 cups cold water
2 tablespoons salt
½ cup vegetable oil, butter, or ghee*
2 tablespoons plain yogurt
½ teaspoon ground saffron threads,* dissolved in 4 tablespoons hot water

In this book the term "spatula" refers to a slotted spatula, as pictured above. However, any large spoon or similar implement will work.

1. Pick over the rice carefully to remove its many small solid particles of grit.

2. Wash the rice by placing it in a large container and covering it with lukewarm water. Agitate gently with your hand, then pour off the water. Repeat five times until the rice is completely clean.

3. In a large nonstick pot, bring 8 cups of water and 2 tablespoons salt to a boil. Add the rice to the pot and boil briskly for 6 to 10 minutes, gently stirring twice with a wooden spoon to loosen any grains that stick to the bottom. Once the rice rises to the top of the pot, it is done.

4. Drain the rice in a large, fine-mesh strainer and rinse with 3 cups lukewarm water.

5. In a bowl, whisk together 4 tablespoons oil, 2 spatulas full of the rice, the yogurt, ½ cup lukewarm water, and 1 tablespoon of saffron water. Spread this mixture over the bottom of the rice pot. This will form the golden crust, or *tah dig*.

6. One spatula full at a time, gently mound the remaining rice onto the *tah dig* layer. Shape it into a pyramid to leave room for the rice's expansion.

7. Cover the pot and cook the rice for 10 minutes over medium heat.

8. Mix 1 cup cold water with 4 tablespoons oil and pour over rice. Sprinkle on the remaining saffron water. Place a clean dishtowel or 2 layers of paper towel over the pot to absorb condensation, and cover with the lid to prevent steam from escaping. Reduce the heat to low and cook 50 minutes longer.

9. Remove the pot from the heat and cool it, still covered, on a damp surface for 5 minutes to loosen the crust.

10. There are two ways to serve the rice. The first is to hold the serving platter tightly over the uncovered pot and invert the two together, unmolding the entire mound onto the platter. The rice will emerge as a golden-crusted cake, to be garnished with edible flowers and herbs, then served in wedges. The second serving style is to spoon the rice into a pyramid on the serving platter, taking care not to disturb the bottom crust as you do so. After the pyramid is shaped, detach the crust with a wooden spatula and arrange it in pieces around the pyramid or serve it on a small side platter. NUSH-E JAN!

Note: You can use any kind of pot to make this rice, but nonstick pots make unmolding the rice much easier.

Note: If using American long-grain rice wash the rice once only.

Note: To reheat leftover rice, place the rice in a saucepan with ½ cup water and place over low heat for 15 to 20 minutes.

Saffron Steamed Plain Basmati Rice

Chelow ba polow paz

SERVINGS: 6
PREP TIME: *10 min.*
COOKING TIME: *1¼ hours*

3 cups long-grain white basmati rice
4 cups cold water
1 tablespoon salt
4 tablespoons vegetable oil, butter, or ghee*
¼ teaspoon ground saffron threads,* dissolved in 1 tablespoon hot water

1. Pick over and wash the rice per the master recipe on page 89.

2. In the rice cooker, combine the rice, water, salt, and oil. Gently stir with a wooden spoon until the salt has dissolved. Start the rice cooker.

3. After 1¼ hours, pour saffron water over the rice. Unplug the rice cooker.

4. Keep the cooker covered and allow it to cool for 10 minutes.

5. Remove the lid, hold the serving platter tightly over the pot and invert the two together, unmolding the entire mound onto the platter. The rice will emerge as a golden-crusted cake, to be garnished with edible flowers and herbs, then served in wedges. *NUSH-E JAN!*

Note: If using American long-grain rice wash the rice once only and use only 3 cups of water in Step 2.

Variation: **Saffron Steamed Brown Basmati Rice**
For 3 cups of brown basmati rice, use 6¾ cups water in Step 2. The amounts of salt, oil, and saffron water remain the same.

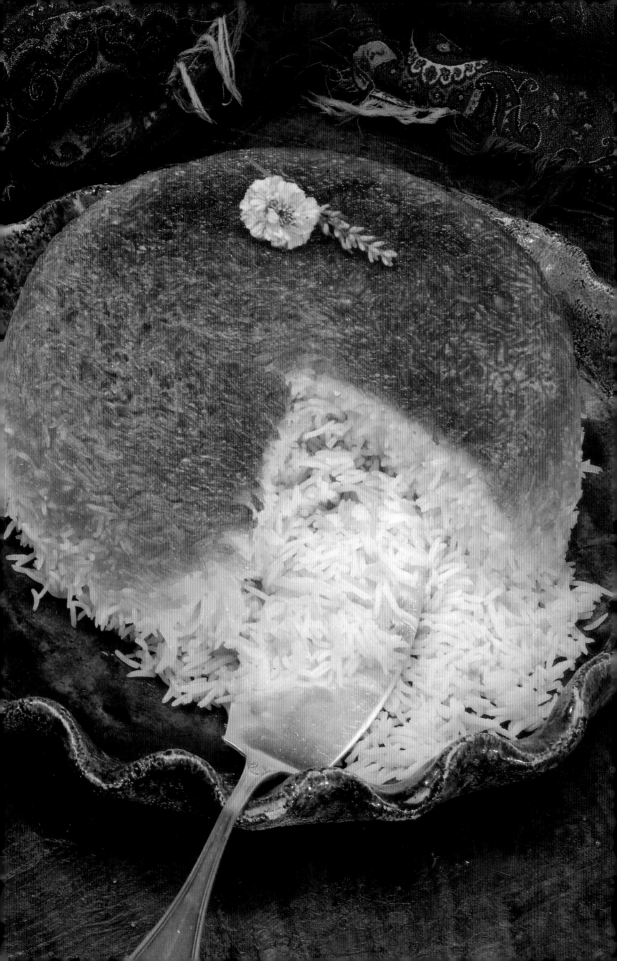

Smothered Rice

Kateh

SERVINGS: 6
PREP TIME: *5 min.*
COOKING TIME: *1¼ hours*

3 cups long-grain white
   basmati rice
5½ cups cold water
1 tablespoon salt
½ cup vegetable oil,
   butter, or ghee*

Most rice in Iran is grown in the Gilan region, near the shores of the Caspian Sea. This recipe is the favored method of cooking rice in Gilan, where it is eaten for breakfast, lunch, and dinner.

1. Pick over and wash the rice per the master recipe on page 89.

2. In a large nonstick pot, combine the rice, water, and salt. Bring to a boil over high heat, then reduce the heat to medium and simmer, uncovered, for 20 minutes. Gently stir twice with a wooden spoon to loosen any grains that stick to the bottom.

3. When the rice has absorbed all the water, pour the oil over it and stir gently with a wooden spoon. Reduce the heat.

4. Place a clean dishtowel or 2 layers of paper towel over the pot to absorb condensation and cover firmly with the lid to prevent steam from escaping. Cook 40 minutes over low heat, taking care that the towel does not burn. Remove the pot from the heat and allow it to cool for 5 minutes on a damp surface without uncovering.

5. Remove the lid, hold the serving platter tightly over the pot and invert the two together, unmolding the entire mound onto the platter. The rice will emerge as a golden-crusted cake, to be garnished with edible flowers and herbs, then served in wedges. NUSH-E JAN!

Note: You can use any kind of pot to make this rice, but nonstick pots make unmolding the rice much easier.

Note: If using American long-grain rice wash the rice once only and use only 4½ cups of water in Step 2.

Jeweled Rice

Javaher polow

SERVINGS: 6
PREP TIME: 40 min.
COOKING TIME: 1½ hours

3 cups long-grain white basmati rice
1 frying chicken (about 3 pounds) or 2 Cornish game hens
2 medium onions, 1 peeled and left whole and 1 peeled and thinly sliced
2 cloves of garlic, peeled
2 teaspoons salt
½ teaspoon freshly ground black pepper
¼ teaspoon ground saffron threads,* dissolved in 2 tablespoons hot water
1 cup very finely slivered orange peel, bitterness removed*
2 large carrots (about ½ pound), peeled and cut into thin strips
1 cup sugar
¾ cup vegetable oil, butter, or ghee*
1 cup dried barberries, cleaned*
½ cup raisins
2 tablespoons plain yogurt
1 teaspoon Persian spice mix (*advieh*)*

GARNISH
2 tablespoons slivered almonds
2 tablespoons slivered unsalted pistachios

Jeweled rice is a festive, sweet dish often served at weddings to bring sweetness to the wedded couple. Each of the elements represents a desirable jewel; for example, barberries stand for rubies, pistachios for emeralds.

1. Preheat oven to 400°F. Stuff the chicken with 1 whole onion, 2 cloves garlic, 1 teaspoon salt, and ½ teaspoon black pepper and place it in a baking dish. Sprinkle with salt and ½ teaspoon saffron water, cover, and bake for 1½ hours at 400°F, basting occasionally. Set aside and keep warm until ready to serve.

2. Meanwhile, place the orange peel, carrot strips, 1 cup sugar, and 1 cup water in a saucepan and boil for 10 minutes. Drain, reserving the liquid, and set aside.

3. In a large skillet, heat 1 tablespoon oil over medium heat and fry the other onion for 15 to 20 minutes, stirring occasionally, until golden brown. Add the barberries and raisins and stir-fry for 1 minute longer. Be careful: Barberries burn very easily. Remove the pan from the heat and set aside.

4. Pick over and wash the rice per the master recipe on page 89. In a large nonstick pot, bring 8 cups of water and 2 tablespoons salt to a boil. Add the rice to the pot and boil briskly for 6 to 10 minutes, gently stirring twice with a wooden spoon to loosen any grains that stick to the bottom. Once the rice rises to the top of the pot, it is done.

5. Drain the rice in a large, fine-mesh strainer and rinse with 3 cups lukewarm water.

6. In a bowl, whisk together 4 tablespoons oil, ½ cup water, 2 spatulas full of the rice, the yogurt, and 1 tablespoon saffron water, and spread the mixture over the bottom of the pot. This will form the golden crust, or *tah dig*.

7. Place 2 spatulas full of rice in the pot. Sprinkle with ½ teaspoon *advieh*. Add a spatula full of the orange peel and carrot mixture. Repeat, alternating layers of rice with the orange peel and carrot, mounding the ingredients in the shape of a pyramid. Sprinkle the remaining *advieh* on top.

8. Cover the pot and cook the rice mixture for 10 minutes over medium heat.

9. Mix 1 cup cold water with 4 tablespoons oil and the liquid reserved in Step 3 and pour over the rice. Sprinkle on the remaining saffron water.

10. Place a clean dish towel or 2 layers of paper towel over the pot to absorb condensation and cover with the lid to prevent steam from escaping. Reduce heat to low and cook 50 minutes longer, taking care that the towel does not burn. Carve the chicken.

11. Remove the pot from the heat and cool it, still covered, on a damp surface for 5 minutes to loosen the crust.

12. Remove the lid, then, gently taking 1 spatula full of rice at a time, place rice on a serving platter in alternating layers with the barberry mixture. Mound the rice in the shape of a cone. Decorate the top of the mound with some barberry mixture, almonds and pistachios. Detach the crust from the bottom of the pot using a wooden spatula. Unmold onto a small platter and serve on the side with the carved chicken. NUSH-E JAN!

Rice with Tomato
Eslamboli polow

SERVINGS: *6*
PREP TIME: *20 min.*
COOKING TIME: *1½ hours*

❧

3 cups long-grain white
  basmati rice
⅔ cup vegetable oil,
  butter, or ghee*
1 large onion, peeled
  and thinly sliced
4 cloves garlic
1 pound skinless,
  boneless chicken, fish
  or meat (lamb, veal,
  beef) cut in 1-inch
  cubes
1 large eggplant (about
  1 pound), peeled and
  sliced with bitterness
  removed*
3 tablespoons tomato
  paste
6 large, fresh tomatoes,
  peeled* and puréed,
  or 6 cups tomato
  purée, or 1 12-ounce
  can whole tomatoes,
  drained and puréed
1 teaspoon salt
½ teaspoon ground
  turmeric
1 teaspoon ground
  cinnamon
1 teaspoon freshly
  ground black pepper
¼ teaspoon ground
  saffron threads,*
  dissolved in 2
  tablespoons hot water

1. Pick over and wash the rice per the master recipe on page 89.

2. In a medium pot, heat 2 tablespoons oil over medium heat. Add the onion and stir-fry for 5 minutes, until translucent. Add the garlic and meat and stir-fry for 10 minutes longer.

3. Add the eggplant to the pot and stir-fry 5 minutes longer. Add the tomato paste, puréed tomatoes, salt, turmeric, cinnamon, and pepper. Cover and simmer over low heat for about 25 minutes.

4. In a large nonstick pot, bring 8 cups of water and 2 tablespoons salt to a boil. Add the rice to the pot and boil briskly for 6 to 10 minutes, gently stirring twice with a wooden spoon to loosen any grains that stick to the bottom. Once the rice rises to the top of the pot, it is done.

5. Drain the rice in a large, fine-mesh strainer and rinse with 3 cups luke-warm water.

6. In a bowl, whisk together 4 tablespoons oil, ½ cup water, 2 spatulas full of rice, and 1 tablespoon saffron water, and spread the mixture over the bottom of the pot. This will form the golden crust, or *tah dig*.

7. Place 2 spatulas full of rice in the pot. Add a spatula full of the tomato and meat mixture. Repeat, alternating layers of rice with tomatoes and meat, mounding the ingredients in the shape of a pyramid.

8. Cover the pot and cook the rice mixture for 10 minutes over medium heat.

9. Mix 2 tablespoons cold water with 4 tablespoons oil and pour over the rice. Sprinkle on the remaining saffron water.

10. Place a clean dishtowel or 2 layers of paper towel over the pot to absorb condensation and cover firmly with the lid to prevent steam from escaping. Reduce the heat to low and cook 40 minutes longer, taking care that the towel does not burn.

11. Remove the pot from the heat and cool it, still covered, on a damp surface for 5 minutes to loosen the crust.

12. Remove the lid, hold the serving platter tightly over the pot, and invert the two together, unmolding the entire mound onto the platter. The rice will emerge as a golden-crusted cake, to be garnished with edible flowers and herbs, then served in wedges. NUSH-E JAN!

Rice with Tomato
Dami-e gojeh farangi

SERVINGS: *6*
PREP TIME: *20 min.*
COOKING TIME: *1¼ hours*

3 cups long-grain white
   basmati rice
3 tablespoons oil,
   butter, or ghee*
1 large onion, peeled
   and thinly sliced
4 cloves garlic
1 large eggplant (about
   1 pound), peeled and
   sliced with bitterness
   removed*
1 large green pepper,
   seeded and sliced
1 pound ground
   chicken, beef, or lamb
1½ tablespoons salt
1 teaspoon freshly
   ground black pepper
½ teaspoon ground
   turmeric
1 teaspoon ground
   cinnamon
¼ teaspoon ground
   saffron threads,*
   dissolved in 2
   tablespoons hot water
4 large, fresh tomatoes,
   peeled* and puréed,
   or 4 cups tomato
   purée, or 1 12-ounce
   can whole tomatoes,
   drained and puréed

This rice cooker method of making Eslamboli polow *uses virtually the same ingredients, but is simpler and less messy to make than the stovetop method. This results in the same combination of flavors as the traditional method but one loses some of the delicacy of seasoning and the sophisticated layered effect. This method can be used for any* polow *recipe using ground meat.*

1. Pick over and wash the rice per the master recipe on page 89.

2. In the rice cooker, heat 3 tablespoons oil and stir-fry the onion, garlic, eggplant, and green pepper for 10 minutes. Add the ground meat and stir-fry 10 minutes, until golden brown.

3. Add the salt, pepper, turmeric, cinnamon, and saffron water, and stir-fry 3 minutes.

4. Stirring gently, add rice and tomato purée. Cover and cook 40 minutes.

5. Unplug the rice cooker and allow to sit for 10 minutes. Remove the lid and place a round serving dish over the pot. Hold the serving dish and pot together tightly and flip them to unmold the rice. The rice will be like a cake. Cut it into slices and serve. NUSH-E JAN!

Variation: Replace the ground meat with 2 pounds of flounder, cut into 1-inch pieces.

Rice with Lentils & Dates

Adas Polow

SERVINGS: 6

SERVINGS: *6*
PREP TIME: *35 min.*
COOKING TIME: *1½ hours*

3 cups long-grain white
   basmati rice
¾ cup vegetable oil,
   butter, or ghee*
2 medium onions,
   peeled and thinly
   sliced
5 cloves garlic, peeled
   and crushed
1 pound skinless,
   boneless chicken or
   meat (lamb, veal, beef)
   cut in 1-inch cubes
1½ teaspoons salt
¼ teaspoon freshly
   ground black pepper
½ teaspoon ground
   turmeric
1 teaspoon ground
   cinnamon
2 teaspoons Persian
   spice mix (*advieh*)*
1 teaspoon ground
   saffron threads,*
   dissolved in 4
   tablespoons hot water
1½ cups green lentils
1 cup raisins
2 cups pitted dates
½ cup slivered orange
   peel, bitterness
   removed*
2 tablespoons plain
   yogurt

1. Pick over and wash the rice per the master recipe on page 89.

2. In a medium pot, heat 2 tablespoons oil over medium heat. Add half the sliced onion and stir-fry for 5 minutes, until translucent. Add the garlic and meat and stir-fry for 10 minutes longer. Add 1 teaspoon salt, the pepper, turmeric, and cinnamon, 1 teaspoon *advieh* and 1½ cups water. Bring to a boil, cover, and simmer for 25 minutes over low heat. Add a few drops of saffron water and set aside.

3. Meanwhile, cook the lentils in 3 cups of water with ½ teaspoon salt for 10 minutes. Drain the lentils, reserving the water for later use, and set aside.

4. In a large skillet heat 2 tablespoons oil over medium heat. Add the remaining onion and fry for 15 to 20 minutes, stirring occasionally, until golden brown. Add the raisins, dates, and slivered orange peel, and stir-fry 2 minutes longer; set aside.

5. In a large nonstick pot, bring 8 cups of water and 2 tablespoons salt to a boil. Add the rice to the pot and boil briskly for 6 to 10 minutes, gently stirring twice with a wooden spoon to loosen any grains that stick to the bottom. Once the rice rises to the top of the pot, it is done.

6. Drain the rice in a large, fine-mesh strainer and rinse with 3 cups lukewarm water.

7. In a bowl, whisk together 4 tablespoons oil, ½ cup water, 2 spatulas full of rice, the yogurt, and 1 tablespoon saffron water, and spread the mixture over the bottom of the pot. This will form the golden crust, or *tah dig*.

8. Place 2 spatulas full of rice in the pot. Sprinkle with ¼ teaspoon *advieh*. Add a spatula full of the lentil mixture and then a spatula full of the meat. Repeat, alternating layers of rice with lentils and meat, mounding the ingredients in the shape of a pyramid. Sprinkle the remaining *advieh* on top.

9. Cover the pot and cook the rice mixture for 10 minutes over medium heat.

10. Mix ¼ cup cold water with 4 tablespoons oil and pour over rice. Sprinkle on the remaining saffron water. Place a clean dishtowel or 2 layers of paper towel over the pot to absorb condensation and cover firmly with the lid to prevent steam from escaping. Reduce the heat to low and cook 50 minutes longer, taking care that the towel does not burn.

11. Remove the pot from the heat and cool it, still covered, on a damp surface for 5 minutes to loosen the crust.

12. Remove the lid, hold the serving platter tightly over the pot, and invert the two together, unmolding the entire mound onto the platter. The rice will emerge as a golden-crusted cake, to be garnished with edible flowers and herbs, then served in wedges. Alternately, you may lift out the rice mixture, taking care not to disturb the *tah dig*, and heap it onto a serving platter, as shown here. Serve the *tah dig* separately on the side. NUSH-E JAN!

Rice with Green Beans & Tomatoes
Lubia polow

SERVINGS: 6
PREP TIME: *45 min.*
COOKING TIME: *1 hour*

3 cups long-grain white
   basmati rice
¾ cup vegetable oil,
   butter, or ghee*
1 large onion, peeled
   and thinly sliced
2 cloves garlic, peeled
   and crushed
1 pound skinless,
   boneless chicken or
   meat (lamb, veal, beef)
   cut in ½-inch cubes
1½ pounds fresh green
   beans, cleaned and cut
   into ½-inch pieces
4 large fresh tomatoes,
   peeled* and sliced, or
   1 pound sliced and
   peeled canned
   tomatoes, drained
1 teaspoon salt
¼ teaspoon freshly
   ground black pepper
½ teaspoon ground
   cinnamon
1 teaspoon Persian spice
   mix (*advieh*)*
1 teaspoon dried
   Persian lime powder*
2 tablespoons plain
   yogurt
½ teaspoon ground
   saffron threads,*
   dissolved in 2
   tablespoons hot water

Green beans and tomatoes came relatively recently to Iran from the New World but quickly gained popularity. This dish was my childhood favorite, and now it has become one of my children's favorite as well.

1. Pick over and wash the rice per the master recipe on page 89.

2. In a medium pot, heat 2 tablespoons oil over medium heat. Add the onion and stir-fry for 5 minutes, until translucent. Add the garlic and meat and stir-fry for 10 minutes longer. Add the green beans and stir-fry 1 minute longer. Add the tomatoes, salt, pepper, cinnamon, *advieh*, and lime powder. Cover and simmer over low heat for 25 minutes.

3. In a large nonstick pot, bring 8 cups of water and 2 tablespoons salt to a boil. Add the rice to the pot and boil briskly for 6 to 10 minutes, gently stirring twice with a wooden spoon to loosen any grains that stick to the bottom. Once the rice rises to the top of the pot, it is done.

4. Drain the rice in a large, fine-mesh strainer and rinse with 3 cups luke-warm water.

5. In a bowl, whisk together 4 tablespoons oil, ½ cup water, 2 spatulas full of rice, the yogurt, and 1 tablespoon saffron water, and spread the mixture over the bottom of the pot. This will form the golden crust, or *tah dig*.

6. Place 2 spatulas full of rice in the pot. Add a spatula full of the bean and meat mixture. Repeat, alternating layers of rice with beans and meat, mounding the ingredients in the shape of a pyramid.

7. Cover the pot and cook the rice mixture for 10 minutes over medium heat.

8. Mix ¼ cup cold water with 4 tablespoons oil and pour over rice. Sprinkle on the remaining saffron water.

9. Place a clean dishtowel or 2 layers of paper towel over the pot to absorb condensation and cover firmly with the lid to prevent steam from escaping. Reduce the heat to low and cook 50 minutes longer, taking care the towel does not burn.

10. Remove the pot from the heat and cool it, still covered, on a damp surface for 5 minutes to loosen the crust.

11. Remove the lid, hold the serving platter tightly over the pot and invert the two together, unmolding the entire mound onto the platter. The rice will emerge as a golden-crusted cake, to be garnished with edible flowers and herbs, then served in wedges. NUSH-E JAN!

Rice with Cabbage & Cumin

Kalam polow

SERVINGS: *6*
PREP TIME: *30 min.*
COOKING TIME: *1½ hours*

3 cups long-grain white
  basmati rice
¾ cup vegetable oil,
  butter, or ghee*
1 medium onion, peeled
  and sliced
1 pound skinless,
  boneless chicken or
  meat (lamb, veal, beef)
  cut in 1-inch cubes
1 large head green
  cabbage, washed and
  cut into 1-inch pieces
½ teaspoon salt
½ teaspoon freshly
  ground black pepper
1 tablespoon ground
  cumin or caraway
  seeds
1 tablespoon Persian
  spice mix (*advieh*)*
6 medium tomatoes,
  peeled* and chopped
  or 1 pound sliced and
  peeled canned
  tomatoes, drained
2 tablespoons plain
  yogurt
1 teaspoon ground
  saffron threads,*
  dissolved in 4
  tablespoons hot water

1. Pick over and wash the rice per the master recipe on page 89.

2. In a medium pot, heat 2 tablespoons oil over medium heat. Add the onion and stir-fry for 5 minutes, until translucent. Add the meat and stir-fry for 10 minutes longer. Add the cabbage and stir-fry 1 minute longer.

3. Add the salt, pepper, ½ tablespoon cumin, ½ tablespoon *advieh*, and the tomatoes. Cover and cook for 25 minutes over low heat.

4. In a large non-stick pot, bring 8 cups of water and 2 tablespoons salt to a boil. Add the rice to the pot and boil briskly for 6 to 10 minutes, gently stirring twice with a wooden spoon to loosen any grains that stick to the bottom. Once the rice rises to the top of the pot, it is done.

5. Drain the rice in a large, fine-mesh strainer and rinse with 3 cups luke-warm water.

6. In a bowl, whisk together 4 tablespoons oil, ½ cup water, 2 spatulas full of rice, the yogurt, and 1 tablespoon saffron water, and spread the mixture over the bottom of the pot. This will form the golden crust, or *tah dig*.

7. Place 2 spatulas full of rice in the pot. Sprinkle with remaining cumin and *advieh*. Add a spatula full of the cabbage and meat mixture. Repeat, alternating layers of rice with cabbage and meat, mounding the ingredients in the shape of a pyramid.

8. Cover the pot and cook the rice mixture for 10 minutes over medium heat.

9. Mix ¼ cup cold water with 4 tablespoons oil and pour over rice. Sprinkle on the remaining saffron water.

10. Place a clean dishtowel or 2 layers of paper towel over the pot to absorb condensation and cover firmly with the lid to prevent steam from escaping. Reduce the heat to low and cook 50 minutes longer, taking care the towel does not burn.

11. Remove the pot from the heat and cool it, still covered, on a damp surface for 5 minutes to loosen the crust.

12. Remove the lid, hold the serving platter tightly over the pot and invert the two together, unmolding the entire mound onto the platter. The rice will emerge as a golden-crusted cake, to be garnished with edible flowers and herbs, then served in wedges. NUSH-E JAN!

Rice with Noodles & Dates
Reshteh polow

SERVINGS: *6*
PREP TIME: *15 min.*
COOKING TIME: *1½ hours*

3 cups long-grain white basmati rice
¾ cup vegetable oil, butter, or ghee*
2 medium onions, peeled and thinly sliced
2 cloves garlic, peeled and crushed
1 pound skinless, boneless chicken or meat (lamb, veal, beef) cut in 1-inch cubes
1 teaspoon salt
½ teaspoon freshly ground black pepper
½ teaspoon ground turmeric
2 teaspoons Persian spice mix (*advieh*)*
1 teaspoon ground saffron threads,* dissolved in 4 tablespoons hot water
½ pound toasted Persian noodles,* cut into 1-inch lengths
½ cup raisins
2 cups pitted dates, cut in half
⅓ cup slivered orange peel, bitterness removed*
2 tablespoons plain yogurt

1. Pick over and wash the rice per the master recipe on page 89.

2. In a medium pot, heat 2 tablespoons oil over medium heat. Add half the sliced onion and stir-fry for 5 minutes, until translucent. Add the garlic and meat and stir-fry for 10 minutes longer. Add 1 teaspoon salt, the pepper and turmeric, 1 teaspoon *advieh*, and 1½ cups water. Bring to a boil, cover, and simmer for 25 minutes over low heat. Add a few drops of saffron water and set aside.

3. Meanwhile, in a large skillet heat 2 tablespoons oil over medium heat. Add the remaining onion and fry for 15 to 20 minutes, stirring occasionally, until golden brown. Add the raisins, dates, and slivered orange peel, and stir-fry 2 minutes longer. Set aside.

4. In a large non-stick pot, bring 10 cups of water and 2 tablespoons salt to a boil. Add the rice and noodles to the pot and boil briskly for 6 to 10 minutes, gently stirring twice with a wooden spoon to loosen any grains that stick to the bottom. Once the rice rises to the top of the pot, it is done.

5. Drain the rice and noodles in a large, fine-mesh strainer and rinse with 3 cups lukewarm water.

6. In a bowl, whisk together 4 tablespoons oil, ½ cup water, 2 spatulas full of rice, the yogurt, and 1 tablespoon saffron water, and spread the mixture over the bottom of the pot. This will form the golden crust, or *tah dig*.

7. Place 2 spatulas full of rice and noodles in the pot. Sprinkle with ½ teaspoon *advieh*. Add a spatula full of the raisin and date mixture and then a spatula full of the meat with its juices. Repeat, alternating layers of rice with layers of the raisin and date mixture and meat, mounding the ingredients in the shape of a pyramid. Sprinkle the remaining *advieh* on top.

8. Cover the pot and cook the rice mixture for 10 minutes over medium heat.

9. Mix ½ cup cold water with 4 tablespoons oil and pour over the rice. Sprinkle on the remaining saffron water.

10. Place a clean dishtowel or 2 layers of paper towel over the pot to absorb condensation and cover firmly with the lid to prevent steam from escaping. Reduce the heat to low and cook 50 minutes longer, taking care that the towel does not burn.

11. Remove the pot from the heat and cool it, still covered, on a damp surface for 5 minutes to loosen the crust.

12. Remove the lid, hold the serving platter tightly over the pot and invert the two together, unmolding the entire mound onto the platter. The rice will emerge as a golden-crusted cake, to be garnished with edible flowers and herbs, then served in wedges. Alternately, you may lift out the rice mixture, taking care not to disturb the *tah dig*, and heap it onto a serving platter, as shown here. Serve the *tah dig* separately on the side. NUSH-E JAN!

Rice with Apricots

Gheisi polow

SERVINGS: *6*
PREP TIME: *15 min.*
COOKING TIME: *1½ hours*

3 cups long-grain white basmati rice
¾ cup vegetable oil, butter, or ghee*
2 medium onions, peeled and thinly sliced
1 pound skinless, boneless chicken or meat (lamb, veal, beef) cut in 1-inch cubes
1 teaspoon salt
½ teaspoon freshly ground black pepper
½ teaspoon ground saffron threads,* dissolved in 2 tablespoons hot water
½ cup raisins
2¼ cups dried apricots, quartered
½ cup pitted dates
1 teaspoon ground cinnamon
¼ teaspoon ground nutmeg
2 tablespoons plain yogurt

Apricots have appeared in Persian cuisine for more than 2,000 years, and this is an ancient recipe. The combination of lamb and apricots is, as my mother used to say, "A good marriage."

1. Pick over and wash the rice per the master recipe on page 89.

2. In a medium pot, heat 2 tablespoons oil over medium heat. Add half the sliced onion and stir-fry for 5 minutes, until translucent. Add meat and stir-fry for 10 minutes longer. Add the salt, pepper, and 1½ cups water. Bring to a boil, cover, and simmer for 25 minutes over low heat. Add a few drops of saffron water and set aside.

3. Meanwhile, in a large skillet, heat 2 tablespoons oil over medium heat. Add the remaining onion and fry for 15 to 20 minutes, stirring occasionally, until golden brown. Add the raisins, apricots, and dates, and stir-fry for 2 minutes longer. Sprinkle the cinnamon and nutmeg on top and set aside.

4. In a large nonstick pot, bring 8 cups of water and 2 tablespoons salt to a boil. Add the rice to the pot and boil briskly for 6 to 10 minutes, gently stirring twice with a wooden spoon to loosen any grains that stick to the bottom. Once the rice rises to the top of the pot, it is done.

5. Drain the rice in a large, fine-mesh strainer and rinse with 3 cups lukewarm water.

6. In a bowl, whisk together 4 tablespoons oil, ½ cup water, 2 spatulas full of rice, the yogurt, and 1 tablespoon saffron water, and spread the mixture over the bottom of the pot. This will form the golden crust, or *tah dig.*

7. Place 2 spatulas full of rice in the pot. Add a spatula full of the meat with its juices and a spatula of the fruit mixture. Repeat, alternating layers of rice with layers of meat and fruit, mounding the ingredients in the shape of a pyramid.

8. Cover the pot and cook the rice mixture for 10 minutes over medium heat.

9. Mix ¼ cup water with 4 tablespoons oil and pour over rice. Sprinkle on the remaining saffron water.

10. Place a clean dishtowel or 2 layers of paper towel over the pot to absorb condensation and cover firmly with the lid to prevent steam from escaping. Reduce the heat to low and cook 50 minutes longer, taking care the towel does not burn.

11. Remove the pot from the heat and cool it, still covered, on a damp surface for 5 minutes to loosen the crust.

12. Remove the lid, hold the serving platter tightly over the pot, and invert the two together, unmolding the entire mound onto the platter. The rice will emerge as a golden-crusted cake, to be garnished with edible flowers and herbs. NUSH-E JAN*!*

Variation: Cook the rice without meat and serve with grilled lamb chops as shown here.

Dill Rice with Fava Beans

Baqala polow

SERVINGS: 6
PREP TIME: *45 min.*
COOKING TIME: *1¼ hours*

RICE

3 cups long-grain white basmati rice

2 pounds fresh fava beans, shelled, or 1 pound frozen*

½ teaspoon turmeric

¾ cup vegetable oil, butter, or ghee*

2 tablespoons plain yogurt

1 teaspoon ground saffron threads,* dissolved in 4 tablespoons hot water

½ cup chopped fresh leeks

5½ cups coarsely chopped fresh dill

½ cup chopped fresh coriander leaves

5 cloves garlic, peeled and crushed or 10 sweet fresh garlic, trimmed*

2 teaspoons ground cinnamon

FISH

1 whole Canadian smoked whitefish, 4 to 5 pounds

4 cloves garlic

1 tablespoon butter

4 Seville oranges, or limes

1 teaspoon salt

½ teaspoon fresh ground pepper

This dish or rice with fresh herbs (sabzi polow) is traditionally served with fish, especially smoked fish, at Nowruz, the Persian New Year. It never fails to remind me of the annual visit of Khanum Rashty, the "lady from Rasht," near the Caspian Sea. She was an old family retainer who would suddenly appear in our garden two weeks before the New Year. There she would be, a short, wiry woman with two gray braids tied on top of her head, her colorful scarf falling down around her neck. She always offered us a large, two-handled wicker basket filled with wonderful spring treasures. Around its edges were bunches of violets, my mother's favorite flower; there was always an enormous bouquet of yellow-centered, double-petaled wild narcissus as well. Within were Seville oranges nestled in their green leaves. And hidden among them, its head and tail peeking out at us, was a large smoked whitefish. This, Khanum Rashty always said, was her New Year's gift to us. My mother saw to it that she was handsomely looked after in return, and we all enjoyed the presents. The flowers filled the house with the scent of spring all through the days that followed. As for the fish, we ate it with the fragrant herb rice of this recipe.

1. Pick over and wash the rice per the master recipe on page 89.

2. Shell and skin the fresh fava beans. Soak frozen ones for a few minutes in warm water for a few minutes, then peel them.

3. In a large nonstick pot, bring 10 cups of water, 3 tablespoons salt and the turmeric to a boil. Add the rice and fava beans to the pot and boil briskly for 6 to 10 minutes, gently stirring twice with a wooden spoon to loosen any grains that stick to the bottom. Once the rice rises to the top of the pot, it is done.

3. Drain the rice and beans in a large, fine-mesh strainer and rinse with 3 cups lukewarm water.

4. In a bowl, whisk together 4 tablespoons oil, ½ cup water, 2 spatulas full of rice, the yogurt, and 1 tablespoon saffron water, and spread the mixture over the bottom of the pot. This will form the golden crust, or *tah dig*.

5. In a large bowl, combine the chopped herbs, garlic, cinnamon, toss well and set aside.

6. Place 2 spatulas full of rice and beans in the pot. Add a spatula full of the herbs and garlic. Repeat, alternating layers of rice and beans with herbs and garlic, mounding the ingredients in the shape of a pyramid.

7. Cover the pot and cook the rice mixture for 10 minutes over medium heat.

8. Mix 1 cup cold water with 4 tablespoons oil and pour over the rice and beans. Sprinkle on the remaining saffron water.

9. Place a clean dishtowel or 2 layers of paper towel over the pot to absorb condensation and cover firmly with the lid to prevent steam from escaping. Reduce the heat to low and cook 50 minutes longer, taking care the towel does not burn.

10. While the rice is cooking, prepare the fish. Preheat the oven to 350°F. Press the garlic, butter, salt, and pepper into the cavity of the fish. Pour in the lime or Seville orange juice. Wrap in parchment or foil. Place it in a baking dish and bake for 45 minutes.

11.Remove the pot from the heat and cool it, still covered, on a damp surface for 5 minutes to loosen the crust.

12. Remove the lid, hold the serving platter tightly over the pot and invert the two together, unmolding the entire mound onto the platter. The rice will emerge as a golden-crusted cake, to be garnished with edible flowers and herbs. When the fish is done, gently remove it from the parchment or foil and transfer it to another serving dish. Garnish with halves of Seville oranges or limes. *NUSH-E JAN!*

Note: This rice dish is delicious with any fish, hot or cold, smoked, fried, baked or grilled. It is also particularly good with lamb.

Sweet Rice with Orange Peel

Shirin polow

SERVINGS: *6*
PREP TIME: *40 min.*
COOKING TIME: *1½ hours*

3 cups long-grain white basmati rice
⅔ cup vegetable oil, butter, or ghee*
1 medium onion, peeled and thinly sliced
1 pound boneless chicken, cut into 1-inch strips
1 teaspoon salt
½ teaspoon freshly ground black pepper
2 large carrots (about ½ pound), peeled and cut into thin strips
2 cups slivered orange peel, bitterness removed*
2 cups sugar
1 cup slivered unsalted pistachios
1 cup slivered almonds, toasted*
1 teaspoon ground saffron threads,* dissolved in 4 tablespoons hot water
1 piece *lavash* bread*
1 teaspoon Persian spice mix (*advieh*)*
1 teaspoon ground cardamom

In this recipe, as in other "sweet rice" recipes such as Albalu polow, *a piece of* lavash *bread is placed between the* tah dig *and the rice. This is to protect the* tah dig *from the sugars, which if allowed to trickle down to the* tah dig, *greatly increases the likelihood of burning the* tah dig *and the pot. In old Persia, a criteria to become a royal chef was to be able to make this recipe without using the* lavash *protection and still have the* tah dig *come out light gold.*

1. Pick over and wash the rice per the master recipe on page 89.

2. In a large skillet, heat 2 tablespoons oil over medium heat. Add the onion and stir-fry for 10 minutes, or until translucent. Add the chicken and stir-fry another 10 minutes, stirring until golden brown. Season with 1 teaspoon salt and ½ teaspoon pepper and stir-fry another 2 minutes. Set aside.

3. In a large skillet, heat 2 tablespoons oil over medium heat. Add the carrots and stir-fry for 5 minutes. Add the orange peel, sugar, and 2 cups water and bring to boil. Reduce the heat, and simmer over medium heat for 10 to 15 minutes. Add the pistachios and almonds to the orange-carrot mixture, drain, reserving the syrup, and set aside.

4. In a large nonstick pot, bring 8 cups of water and 2 tablespoons salt to a boil. Add the rice to the pot and boil briskly for 6 to 10 minutes, gently stirring twice with a wooden spoon to loosen any grains that stick to the bottom. Once the rice rises to the top of the pot, it is done.

5. Drain the rice in a large, fine-mesh strainer and rinse with 3 cups lukewarm water.

6. In a bowl, whisk together 4 tablespoons oil, ½ cup water, 2 spatulas full of rice, and 1 tablespoon saffron water, and spread the mixture over the bottom of the pot. This will form the golden crust, or *tah dig*.

7. Cut a piece of *lavash* bread to fit the bottom of the pot. Place the piece of *lavash* so that it rests evenly on top of the *tah dig*.

8. Place 2 spatulas full of rice in the pot. Add a spatula full of the carrot and orange mixture, and then a spatula full of the chicken. Repeat, alternating layers of rice with the carrot mixture and chicken, mounding the rice in the shape of a pyramid. Sprinkle the *advieh* and cardamom on each layer of rice.

9. Cover the pot and cook the rice mixture for 10 minutes over medium heat.

10. Mix 1 cup cold water with 4 tablespoons oil and pour over rice. Drizzle on the remaining saffron water and the syrup reserved in Step 3.

11. Place a clean dishtowel or 2 layers of paper towel over the pot to absorb condensation and cover firmly with the lid to prevent steam from escaping. Reduce the heat to low and cook 50 minutes longer, taking care that the towel does not burn.

13. Remove the pot from the heat and cool it, still covered, on a damp surface for 5 minutes to loosen the crust.

14. Gently taking 1 spatula full of rice at a time, place it on the serving platter. Be careful not to disturb the crust on the bottom of the pot. Mound the rice in the shape of a cone.

15. Detach the crust from the bottom of the pot using a wooden spatula. Unmold onto a small platter and serve on the side. Garnish with lemons or limes if you like. *NUSH-E JAN!*

Variation: This dish can also be made with small, hazelnut-sized meatballs.

Rice with Tart Cherries

Albalu polow

SERVINGS: *6*
PREP TIME: *35 min.*
COOKING TIME: *1½ hours*

3 cups long-grain white basmati rice
1 pound ground beef
2 medium peeled onions, one grated and one thinly sliced
1 teaspoon salt
½ teaspoon freshly ground black pepper
1 teaspoon cinnamon
1 teaspoon ground saffron threads,* dissolved in 2 tablespoons hot water
4 cups pitted dried tart cherries*
1 cup sugar
2 tablespoons lime juice
⅔ cup vegetable oil, butter, or ghee*
1 piece *lavash* bread*
2 tablespoons slivered, toasted almonds•
2 tablespoons slivered pistachios

This dish, traditionally made in the summer with fresh tart (also called sour) cherries, fragile and hard to find these days, always brings back memories. In Iran fresh tart cherries arrived from an orchard in wooden crates, glowing red between their green leaves. The crates were placed in the garden by the stone fountain and gently sprinkled with water to wash off the dust. Then they were transferred to brown wicker baskets to be ready for jam making. But my three sisters and I saw to it that only half became jam. We soaked all our senses in sour cherries: We hung double-stemmed ones over our ears for earrings; we pinned clusters to our clothes for brooches; we squeezed the juice onto our lips to make them red. And of course we ate them, masses of them, fresh, juicy, and luscious. We feasted on cherries. At lunch there would be rice with sour cherries and small meatballs; in the afternoon we dropped spoonfuls of the freshly made jam into our tea; and in the evening we mixed the jam with yogurt to make a wonderful dessert.

1. Pick over and wash the rice per the master recipe on page 89.

2. In a bowl combine the ground beef and grated onion with ½ teaspoon salt, ¼ teaspoon pepper, and ¼ teaspoon cinnamon. Knead well and form into meatballs the size of hazelnuts.

3. In a large skillet heat 1 tablespoon oil over medium heat and carefully add the meatballs. Swirl and shake the pan gently for about 10 minutes—a spatula might break the meatballs—until the meatballs are brown. Add a drop of saffron water, swirl the pan once more, and set aside.

4. In a saucepan, combine the dried cherries, sugar, and 2 cups water. Boil over medium heat for 20 minutes. Stir in the lime juice. Drain, reserving about 1 cup syrup. Add 2 tablespoons oil and the rest of the cinnamon, mix well, and set aside.

5. Bring 8 cups of water and 2 tablespoons salt to a boil in a large non-stick pot. Add the rice to the pot and boil briskly for 6 to 10 minutes, stirring twice with a wooden spoon to loosen any grains that stick. Once the rice rises to the top of the pot, it is done.

6. Drain the rice in a large, fine-mesh strainer and rinse with 3 cups luke-warm water.

7. In a bowl, whisk together 4 tablespoons oil, ½ cup water, and 1 table-spoon saffron water, and pour the mixture over the bottom of the pot. This will help form the golden crust, or *tah dig*.

8. Cut a piece of *lavash* bread to fit the pot, and lay it over the *tah dig* mixture.

9. Place 2 spatulas full of rice in the pot. Add a spatula full of cherries and a spatula full of meatballs. Repeat, alternating layers of rice, cherries, and meatballs. Mound the ingredients in the shape of a cone.

10. Cover the pot and cook the rice mixture for 10 minutes over medium heat.

11. Mix 1 cup cold water with 2 tablespoons oil and pour over the rice.

Sprinkle on the remaining saffron water.

12. Place a dishtowel or 2 layers of paper towel over the pot to absorb condensation; cover firmly with the lid to prevent steam from escaping. Cook 40 minutes longer over low heat, taking care the towel does not burn.

13. Remove the lid and trickle the syrup from Step 4 and 2 tablespoons oil over the rice. Cover and cook another 10 minutes over low heat.

14. Remove pot from the heat and cool it, covered, on a damp surface for 5 minutes to loosen the crust.

15. Without disturbing the *tah dig*, spoon the rice mixture into a serving dish and garnish with 1 table-spoon toasted, slivered almonds and 1 tablespoon toasted, slivered pistachios.* Lift the *tah dig* from the pot and serve it separately. *NUSH-E JAN!*

Barberry Rice

Zereshk polow

SERVINGS: 6
PREP TIME: *40 min.*
COOKING TIME: *1½ hours*

3 cups long-grain white basmati rice
1 frying chicken (about 3 pounds) or 2 Cornish game hens
2 medium onions, 1 peeled and left whole and 1 peeled and thinly sliced
2 cloves garlic, peeled
2 teaspoons salt
½ teaspoon freshly ground black pepper
1 teaspoon ground saffron threads,* dissolved in 4 tablespoons hot water
⅔ cup vegetable oil, butter, or ghee*
2 cups dried barberries, cleaned*
4 tablespoons sugar
2 tablespoons plain yogurt
2 tablespoons cumin seeds
2 tablespoons toasted, slivered almonds for garnish
2 tablespoons slivered unsalted pistachios for garnish

Barberries are an ancient berry; Iran is one of the few countries in the world where they are still used regularly in cooking.

1. Pick over and wash the rice per the master recipe on page 89. Preheat oven to 400°F.

2. Stuff the chicken with the whole onion, garlic, 1 teaspoon salt, ½ teaspoon pepper, and place it in a baking dish. Sprinkle with salt, pepper, and 1 teaspoon saffron water, cover, and bake for 1½ hours at 400°F. Carve and keep warm until ready to serve.

3. In a medium pot, heat 2 tablespoons oil over medium heat. Add the sliced onion and fry for 15 minutes, stirring occasionally, until golden brown. Reduce the heat, add the barberries and sugar, stir-fry 1 minute longer, and set aside. Be careful: Barberries burn very easily.

4. In a large nonstick pot, bring 8 cups of water and 2 tablespoons salt to a boil. Add the rice to the pot and boil briskly for 6 to 10 minutes, gently stirring twice with a wooden spoon to loosen any grains that stick to the bottom. Once the rice rises to the top of the pot, it is done.

5. Drain the rice in a large, fine-mesh strainer and rinse with 3 cups luke-warm water.

6. In a bowl, whisk together 4 tablespoons oil, ½ cup water, 2 spatulas full of rice, the yogurt, and 1 tablespoon saffron water and spread the mixture over the bottom of the pot. This will form the golden crust, or *tah dig*.

7. Place 2 spatulas full of rice in the pot. Continue transferring rice, mounding it into the shape of a pyramid. Sprinkle each layer with cumin.

8. Cover the pot and cook the rice mixture for 10 minutes over medium heat.

9. Mix 1 cup cold water with 4 tablespoons oil and pour over the rice. Sprinkle on the remaining saffron water.

10. Place a clean dishtowel or 2 layers of paper towel over the pot to absorb condensation and cover firmly with the lid to prevent steam from escaping. Reduce the heat to low and cook 50 minutes longer, taking care the towel does not burn.

11. Remove the pot from the heat and cool it, still covered, on a damp surface for 5 minutes to loosen the crust.

12. Then, gently taking 1 spatula full of rice at a time, place the rice on a serving platter in alternating layers with the barberry mixture. Mound the rice in the shape of a cone. Arrange the chicken around the platter. Finally, decorate the top of the mound with some of the barberry mixture, almonds and pistachios. Serve the *tah dig* on the side. NUSH-E JAN!

Note: You may place the barberries in the rice and steam them together but the color of barberries will not be as red as when you layer them with the rice at the last minute.

Golden Crusted Saffron Rice Mold
Tah chin-e bareh

SERVINGS: *8*
PREP TIME: *35 min.*
COOKING TIME: *1½ hours*

1 cup vegetable oil,
  butter, or ghee*
2 large onions, peeled
  and thinly sliced
1 pound skinless,
  boneless lamb,
  chicken or fish cut in
  1-inch strips
2 cloves garlic, peeled
  and crushed
1 tablespoon cumin
  seeds
2 teaspoons salt
1 teaspoon freshly
  ground black pepper
3 cups long-grain white
  basmati rice
1 egg
2½ cups plain yogurt
1 teaspoon ground
  saffron threads,*
  dissolved in 4
  tablespoons hot water
¼ cup candied orange
  peel*

This is a festive peasant dish, often made with an entire baby lamb. The word tah *means "bottom,"* chin *means "to layer" and* bareh *means "lamb."*

1. In a large skillet, heat 2 tablespoons oil over medium heat. Add the onion and stir fry for 10 minutes or until the onion is translucent. Add the meat and garlic and stir-fry for another 10 minutes, until golden brown. Add cumin seeds, 1 teaspoon salt, ½ teaspoon pepper, stir fry for another 2 minutes. Set aside and allow to cool.

2. Pick over and wash the rice per the master recipe on page 89. In a large nonstick pot bring 8 cups of water and 2 tablespoons of salt to a boil. Add the rice to the pot and boil briskly for 6 minutes, gently stirring twice with a wooden spoon to loosen any grains that stick to the bottom of the pot. Once the rice rises to the top, it is done. Drain the rice and rinse it with 3 cups of lukewarm water.

3. Preheat the oven to 400°F.

4. In a large mixing bowl, beat the egg, yogurt, 2 tablespoons of oil, saffron water, candied orange peel, 1 teaspoon salt, and ½ teaspoon pepper, and mix thoroughly for 1 minute.

5. Add the cooked rice to the yogurt mixture and gently mix thoroughly.

6. In a large Pyrex baking dish or two small round ones, heat ¾ cup oil in the oven. Add half of the rice mixture, spreading it across the bottom and up the sides of the baking dish. Place the meat pieces on top, and cover with the rest of the rice. Pack firmly, using a wooden spoon, and cover with oiled aluminum foil or lid.

7. Place the baking dish in the oven and bake 1¼ to 1½ hours, until the bottom turns golden brown.

8. Remove the baking dish from the oven and allow to cool, still covered, on a damp surface for 10 minutes to loosen the crust.

9. Remove the lid and loosen the edges with a knife, hold the serving platter tightly over the baking dish and invert the two together, unmolding the entire mound onto the platter. The rice will emerge as a golden-crusted cake, to be garnished with edible flowers and herbs, then served in wedges. *NUSH-E JAN!*

Khoreshes

Fresh Herb Khoresh

Eggplant Khoresh

Celery & Mint Khoresh

Sweet & Sour Carrot Khoresh

Pomegranate Khoresh

Green Bean & Tomato Khoresh

Potato Khoresh with Orange Peel

Yogurt Khoresh

Rhubarb Khoresh

Butternut Squash Khoresh

Orange Khoresh

Peach Khoresh

Apple Khoresh

KHORESHES

Few dishes are so evocative of the Persian love of fragrance as the delicate braise known as *khoresh*. The one I remember most from my childhood is *Qormeh sabzi* (fresh herb khoresh, page 118). Its preparation would begin early in the morning when, while picking up *barbari* bread for breakfast, we would visit the market to buy the fresh herbs: parsley, chives, coriander, and most important because of the scent, fenugreek. Then all the women of the house would gather around a table with a large copper basin and tray on it. There they chatted companionably while they cleaned and washed the herbs before arranging them in flat woven baskets and setting them in the sun to dry. My mother, who emphasized the importance of even, clean chopping, would do it alone. She would stand over a large oak chopping board, seize a handful of each herb in one hand and with a large cleaver and a rhythmic, fast, even, slanting stroke, set to work. I can see and smell and hear it still: the various greens of the herbs, the sharp steel of the cleaver with droplets of herb juice on it, the lovely aroma, the faraway, trancelike concentration on my mother's angelic face, her strong body adorned with a turquoise necklace—she never wore her rings when she cooked—the even, quick blows of the cleaver. Never was I allowed to try it. It was too dangerous, she said: The time to do this would be when I grew up.

After the herbs were chopped, they were stir-fried, their heavenly scent drifting through the house and even across the neighborhood. Then the other ingredients added their own notes—the lamb we always used in this dish, the onion, the garlic, and the saffron, added at the end to preserve its scent, and finally the gnarled whole dried limes. All the morning the stew would simmer, perfuming our house until lunchtime. I recall those days every time I visit people who are making this dish, especially if they live in apartment buildings: The haunting scent greets us in the elevator and drifts up long corridors, drawing us to friends' doors.

Such a herb *khoresh* is one of many variations on a theme. The dish is really a delicate stew made by combining poultry, meats, or fish with vegetables, fresh or dried fruits, beans, grains, and subtle herbs and spices—whatever is best in season. In the recipes that follow, I have suggested chicken or meat as a base. For the best results, use free-range chicken (I have found "Bell and Evans" chickens to be excellent), battery-raised chicken has almost no flavor. For special occasions, lamb legs or shanks or beef eye of round makes an incomparable stew. For these recipes, however, I have used boneless chicken breast or beef sirloin, cut into small pieces to accelerate cooking. If you use larger or tougher cuts or meat with the bone in, you must adjust cooking times accordingly. You should brown the meat and onions slowly and well, keep water to the minimum needed, and simmer the stew very slowly over very low heat in a heavy pot. While advance cooking doesn't affect chicken-based *khoresh* much, a meat-based version will improve if you make it a day in advance and reheat it just before serving.

Whatever *khoresh* you choose, serve it with *chelow* (saffron steamed rice, pages 89-90): Heap the rice on each plate, place a piece of the golden crust (*tah dig*) on it, and serve the *khoresh* on top. In Iran, this is called *chelow-khoresh*.

Fresh Herb Khoresh
Khoresh-e qormeh sabzi

SERVINGS: *4*
PREP TIME: *25 min.*
COOKING TIME: *1½ hours*

6 tablespoons vegetable oil, butter, or ghee*
2 small onions, peeled and thinly sliced
2 cloves garlic, peeled and crushed
1 pound skinless, boneless chicken leg or meat (lamb, veal, beef), cut into thin strips
1½ teaspoons salt
1 teaspoon freshly ground black pepper
1 teaspoon ground turmeric
½ teaspoon ground saffron threads,* dissolved in 1 tablespoon hot water
4 whole dried Persian limes,* pierced
½ cup dried kidney beans soaked in 2 cups of water for at least 2 hours and drained
4 cups finely chopped fresh parsley
1 cup finely chopped fresh leeks, garlic chives, or scallions
1 cup finely chopped fresh coriander
1 cup chopped fresh fenugreek leaves or 3 tablespoons dried fenugreek sprinkled with water
2 tablespoons dried Persian lime powder* or 4 tablespoons fresh lime or lemon juice

This khoresh *is very popular by the Caspian Sea, where they often make it with fish instead of meat.*

1. In a medium pot, heat 3 tablespoons oil over medium heat. Add the onions and stir-fry 5 minutes, until translucent. Add the garlic and meat, and fry 20 minutes longer, stirring occasionally, until golden brown. Add the salt, pepper, turmeric, saffron water, whole dried Persian limes, and kidney beans, and stir-fry 2 minutes longer.

2. Pour in 4½ cups water and bring to a boil. Reduce the heat to low, cover, and simmer for 30 minutes, stirring occasionally.

3. Meanwhile, in a large skillet heat 3 tablespoons oil over medium heat. Add the chopped parsley, leeks, coriander, and fenugreek, and fry for 20 minutes, stirring occasionally, until the aroma of frying herbs rises. (This stage is very important to the taste of the stew.)

4. Add the sautéed herbs and lime powder or juice to the pot. Cover and simmer over low heat for 30 to 40 minutes longer, until the beans and meat are tender, stirring occasionally.

5. Check to see whether the meat and kidney beans are tender. Taste the stew and adjust the seasoning. Cover and keep warm until ready to serve.

6. Serve hot with saffron steamed rice (*chelow*, pages 89-90). NUSH-E JAN!

Variation: Instead of using meat you can use fillets of firm fish, such as sea bass. Sauté the fish separately and add it to the *khoresh* in Step 5.

Eggplant Khoresh

Khoresh-e bademjan

SERVINGS: *4*
PREP TIME: *20 min.*
COOKING TIME: *1½ hours*

5 tablespoons vegetable oil, butter, or ghee*

3 small onions, peeled and thinly sliced

2 cloves garlic, peeled and crushed

1 pound skinless, boneless chicken or meat (lamb, veal, beef), cut into thin strips

1 teaspoon salt

1 teaspoon freshly ground black pepper

½ teaspoon ground saffron threads,* dissolved in 4 tablespoons hot water

½ teaspoon ground turmeric

3 cups fresh or canned puréed tomatoes (about 6 tomatoes)

1 cup unripe grapes* or 4 tablespoons fresh lime juice

3 medium eggplants (about 2 pounds), peeled and sliced, with bitterness removed*

2 egg whites, lightly beaten

GARNISH
1 tablespoon oil
1 whole small tomato

A golden memory from my childhood is the frying of the eggplant for this khoresh. *My mother would cut the long, thin eggplants lengthwise into precise ¼-inch strips, careful not to cut off the heads. She would then fry them, gently and with great care, to achieve just the right golden color. One of the pleasures of being around the kitchen at eleven in the morning was that she would mockingly scold me for being too skinny (she should see me now) and insist that I join her and eat one of the strips of eggplant on a piece of* sangak *bread as a snack Then she would put her feet up and take a break under the vine-trellis with some tea and one of her two cigarettes of the day. The eggplants would then be laid gently, with their heads sticking out among the bright red tomatoes and other ingredients, in the casserole and cooked with the* khoresh. *While everyone was enjoying the* khoresh *at lunch, and singing its praises, my mother and I would look at each other knowing that we had had the best of it.*

1. In a medium pot, heat 3 tablespoons oil over medium heat. Add the onion and stir-fry 5 minutes, until translucent. Add the garlic and chicken and fry 15 minutes longer, stirring occasionally, until golden brown. Add the salt, pepper, saffron water, and turmeric.

2. Pour in the tomato purée, and unripe grapes and bring to a boil. Reduce the heat to low, cover, and simmer for 15 minutes.

3. Meanwhile, peel the eggplants and cut them length-wise into quarters if they are large and remove the bitterness.* Brush each side of the eggplant pieces with egg white to reduce the oil needed for frying.

4. In a skillet, heat 2 tablespoons oil over medium heat. Add the eggplant and fry for 10 minutes, until all sides are golden brown. Place the eggplant on paper towels to drain and set aside.

5. Meanwhile, prepare the garnish: In the same skillet, heat 1 tablespoon oil over medium heat. Sauté the whole tomato briefly and set it aside.

6. Preheat the oven to 350°F. Transfer the chicken and sauce to a deep ovenproof casserole; arrange the eggplant and tomato on the top. Cover and bake for 30 minutes, then remove cover and bake 15 minutes longer.

7. Adjust the seasoning for salt or lime juice, cover, and keep warm in the oven until ready to serve.

8. Serve hot with saffron steamed rice (*chelow,* pages 89-90). NUSH-E JAN!

Celery & Mint Khoresh

Khoresh-e karafs

SERVINGS: *4*
PREP TIME: *30 min.*
COOKING TIME: *1½ hours*

4 tablespoons vegetable
  oil, butter, or ghee*
5 stalks celery, washed
  and chopped into 1-
  inch lengths (4 cups
  chopped)
3 cups chopped fresh
  parsley
½ cup chopped fresh
  mint or 2 tablespoons
  dried
2 small onions, peeled
  and thinly sliced
1 pound skinless,
  boneless chicken or
  meat (lamb, veal, beef),
  cut into thin strips
2 cloves garlic, peeled
  and crushed
1 teaspoon salt
½ teaspoon freshly
  ground black pepper
½ teaspoon ground
  turmeric
¼ cup fresh lime juice
½ teaspoon ground
  saffron threads,*
  dissolved in 2
  tablespoons hot water
  (optional)

1. In a large skillet, heat 2 tablespoons of oil over medium heat. Add the celery and stir-fry 10 minutes. Add the chopped parsley and mint and stir-fry 10 minutes longer. Set aside.

2. In a medium pot, heat 2 tablespoons oil over medium heat. Add the onions and stir-fry 5 minutes, until translucent. Add the chicken and garlic and fry 15 minutes, stirring occasionally, until golden brown. Add the celery, salt, pepper, turmeric, lime juice, and saffron water and stir-fry 1 minute longer.

3. Pour in 2½ cups water and bring to a boil. Cover, reduce the heat to low, and simmer for 40 minutes.

4. Taste the *khoresh* and adjust the seasoning for salt and lime juice. Cover and keep warm until ready to serve.

5. Serve hot with saffron steamed rice (*chelow*, pages 89-90). NUSH-E JAN!

Sweet & Sour Carrot Khoresh

Khoresh-e havij

SERVINGS: *4*
PREP TIME: *10 min.*
COOKING TIME: *1 hour*

3 tablespoons vegetable oil, butter, or ghee*
2 small onions, peeled and thinly sliced
1 pound skinless, boneless chicken or meat (lamb, veal, beef), cut into thin strips
4 large carrots (about 1 pound), peeled and sliced
1 teaspoon salt
1 teaspoon freshly ground black pepper
1 teaspoon ground cinnamon
¼ teaspoon ground saffron threads,* dissolved in 1 tablespoon hot water (optional)
1 cup sugar
½ cup fresh lime juice
2 tablespoons wine vinegar
1 cup pitted prunes

1. In a medium pot heat the oil over medium heat. Add the onions and stir-fry 5 minutes, until translucent. Add the chicken and fry 15 minutes longer, stirring occasionally, until golden brown. Add the carrots and stir-fry 5 minutes. Add the salt, pepper, cinnamon, saffron water, and stir-fry 1 minute more.

2. Add 2½ cups water, the sugar, lime juice, vinegar, and prunes and bring to a boil. Reduce the heat to low, cover, and simmer for 30 minutes, stirring occasionally.

3. Check the chicken and carrots for tenderness. Taste the *khoresh* and adjust the seasoning for salt and lime juice. Cover and keep warm until ready to serve.

4. Serve hot with saffron steamed rice (*chelow*, pages 89-90). NUSH-E JAN!

Pomegranate Khoresh

Khoresh-e fesenjan

SERVINGS: *4*
PREP TIME: *30 min.*
COOKING TIME: *1 hour*

2 tablespoons vegetable
  oil, butter, or ghee*
2 small onions, peeled
  and thinly sliced
1 pound skinless and
  boneless chicken or
  duck breast cut into
  thin strips
2 large carrots or 1
  pound butternut
  squash, peeled and cut
  into thin strips
½ pound shelled
  walnuts, toasted*
1 teaspoon salt
½ cup pomegranate
  paste* diluted in 2½
  cups water or 4 cups
  fresh pomegranate
  juice*
2 tablespoons sugar
½ teaspoon cinnamon
¼ teaspoon ground
  saffron threads,*
  dissolved in 1
  tablespoon hot water
  (optional)

GARNISH
1 cup fresh
  pomegranate seeds*
¼ cup walnuts, toasted*

Traditionally this recipe is made with duck: The affinity between pomegranate and duck goes back to ancient times in Persia. Fourth-century Persian manuals describe the domestication of the male duck, fed on hemp seeds and the butter of olives. The finest meal possible was one of these ducks served in a pomegranate sauce. This recipe recreates that ancient dish.

1. In a medium pot, heat the oil over medium heat. Add the onions and stir-fry 5 minutes, until translucent. Add the chicken and fry for 15 minutes, stirring occasionally, until golden brown. Add the carrot strips and stir-fry 2 minutes longer.

2. Finely grind the toasted walnuts in a food processor. Add the salt, diluted pomegranate paste, sugar, cinnamon, and saffron water and mix well to create a smooth, creamy sauce. Transfer the sauce to the pot, cover and simmer for 40 minutes over very low heat, stirring occasionally with a wooden spoon to prevent the nuts from burning.

3. Taste the sauce and adjust for seasoning and thickness. This *khoresh* should be sweet and sour, and the consistency of heavy cream. Add diluted pomegranate paste for sourness or sugar for sweetness. If the sauce is too thick, thin it with warm water.

4. Cover and keep warm until ready to serve.

5. Serve hot with saffron steamed rice (*chelow*, pages 89-90). NUSH-E JAN!

Green Bean & Tomato Khoresh

Khoresh-e lubia sabz

SERVINGS: *4*
PREP TIME: *20 min.*
COOKING TIME: *1 hour*

5 tablespoons vegetable oil, butter, or ghee*
1 pound fresh or frozen green beans, washed and trimmed, cut into 2-inch pieces
2 small onions, peeled and thinly sliced
2 cloves garlic, peeled and crushed
1 pound skinless, boneless chicken leg or meat (lamb, veal, beef), cut into thin strips
1 teaspoon salt
1 teaspoon freshly ground black pepper
1 teaspoon ground cinnamon
½ teaspoon ground turmeric
3½ cups fresh or canned puréed tomatoes (about 6 large tomatoes)
1 tablespoon tomato paste
2 tablespoons fresh lime juice
½ teaspoon ground saffron threads,* dissolved in 2 tablespoons hot water (optional)

1. In a large skillet heat 2 tablespoons oil over medium heat. Add the green beans and stir-fry 5 minutes. Remove from the heat and set aside.

2. In a medium pot, heat 3 tablespoons oil over medium heat. Add the onion and stir-fry 5 minutes, until translucent. Add the garlic and chicken and fry 15 minutes, stirring occasionally, until golden brown. Add the salt, pepper, cinnamon, and turmeric and stir-fry 1 minute longer.

3. Add the green beans, tomato purée and paste, lime juice, and saffron water to the pot. Bring to a boil, reduce the heat to low, cover, and simmer for about 30 minutes, or until the beans are tender, stirring occasionally.

4. Taste the *khoresh* and adjust the seasoning for salt and lime juice. Cover and keep warm until ready to serve.

5. Serve hot with saffron steamed rice (*chelow*, pages 89-90). NUSH-E JAN!

Potato Khoresh with Orange Peel
Khoresh-e qeymeh

SERVINGS: *4*
PREP TIME: *20 min.*
COOKING TIME: *1½ hours*

6 tablespoons vegetable
  oil, butter, or ghee*
2 small onions, peeled
  and thinly sliced
1 pound skinless,
  boneless chicken or
  meat (lamb, veal, beef),
  cut into thin strips
4 whole dried Persian
  limes,* pierced or 4
  tablespoons fresh lime
  juice
1 teaspoon salt
1 teaspoon freshly
  ground black pepper
½ teaspoon ground
  turmeric
4 large fresh tomatoes
  or 2 cups puréed
  tomato
⅓ cup yellow split peas*
1 teaspoon Persian spice
  mix (*advieh*)*
2 tablespoons chopped
  candied orange peel*
1 teaspoon ground
  saffron threads,*
  dissolved in 4
  tablespoons hot water
  (optional)
2 tablespoons fresh lime
  juice
1 pound potatoes,
  peeled and cut into
  French-fry-sized sticks

1. In a medium pot heat 4 tablespoons oil over medium heat. Add the onions and stir-fry 5 minutes, until translucent. Add the meat and fry 15 minutes longer, stirring occasionally, until golden brown. Add the dried Persian limes, salt, pepper, and turmeric, and stir-fry 20 seconds longer.

2. Add the tomato purée and 2 cups water and bring to a boil. Cover and simmer over low heat for 10 minutes.

3. Add the yellow split peas, *advieh*, candied orange peel, saffron water, and lime juice. Cover and simmer 30 to 45 minutes, until the meat is tender.

4. Meanwhile, in a large skillet, heat 2 tablespoons oil over medium heat. Add the potatoes and fry for 15 to 20 minutes over medium heat, stirring occasionally, until golden brown. Remove the skillet from the heat. Drain the potatoes and set aside.

5. Check the meat and split peas for tenderness. Adjust salt and pepper to taste. Cover and keep warm until ready to serve.

6. Just before serving, arrange the fried potatoes on top of the *khoresh*. Serve hot with saffron steamed rice (*chelow*, pages 89-90) and fresh vegetables and herbs. NUSH-E JAN!

Yogurt Khoresh

Khoresh-e mast

SERVINGS: *4*
PREP TIME: *15 min.*
COOKING TIME: *1¾ hours*

4 tablespoons vegetable
  oil, butter, or ghee*
2 small onions, peeled
  and thinly sliced
1 pound skinless,
  boneless chicken or
  meat (lamb, veal, beef),
  cut into thin strips
¾ cup chopped celery
1½ teaspoons salt
1 teaspoon freshly
  ground black pepper
2 tablespoons curry
  powder
2 tablespoons fresh lime
  juice
2 cups plain yogurt
1 teaspoon corn starch
  dissolved in ¼ cup
  cold water

GARNISH
¼ cup slivered almonds,
  toasted*
¼ cup raisins or edible
  flowers

1. In a medium pot, heat 4 tablespoons oil over medium heat. Add the onions and stir-fry 5 minutes, until translucent. Add the chicken and celery and fry for 15 minutes longer, stirring occasionally, until golden brown. Add 1 teaspoon salt, the pepper, curry powder, and lime juice. Stir-fry 1 minute longer.

2. Add 1 cup water and bring to a boil. Reduce the heat to low, cover and simmer for 30 minutes, stirring occasionally.

3. In a mixing bowl combine the yogurt, ½ teaspoon salt, and the dissolved corn starch. Beat clockwise for 5 minutes, to prevent curdling.

4. When the chicken is cooked, just before serving, stir in the yogurt and heat very gently for 5 minutes. Do not let the mixture come to a boil.

5. Check the chicken for tenderness. Adjust the seasoning. Cover and keep warm until ready to serve.

6. Garnish with almonds and raisins, or edible flowers, and serve hot with saffron steamed rice (*chelow*, pages 89-90). NUSH-E JAN!

Variation: The curry powder and celery may be replaced by ½ cup candied orange peel* and 1 teaspoon ground saffron threads dissolved in 1 cup hot water. Add the candied orange peel in Step 1; mix the saffron with the yogurt in Step 3.

Rhubarb Khoresh

Khoresh-e rivas

SERVINGS: *4*
PREP TIME: *30 min.*
COOKING TIME: *1½ hours*

4 tablespoons vegetable oil, butter, or ghee*
2 small onions, peeled and thinly sliced
1 pound skinless, boneless chicken or meat (lamb, veal, beef), cut into thin strips
1 teaspoon salt
¼ teaspoon freshly ground black pepper
¼ teaspoon ground turmeric
3 cups chopped fresh parsley
½ cup chopped fresh mint or 2 tablespoons dried
¼ teaspoon ground saffron threads,* dissolved in 1 tablespoon hot water (optional)
1 tablespoon tomato paste
2 tablespoons fresh lime juice
1 pound fresh or frozen rhubarb, cut into 2-inch pieces

In Iran, rhubarb has been reputed since ancient times to cleanse the blood and purify the system.

1. In a medium pot, heat 2 tablespoons oil over medium heat. Add the onions and stir-fry 5 minutes, until translucent. Add the chicken and fry for 15 minutes, stirring occasionally, until golden brown. Add the salt, pepper, and turmeric.

2. Pour in 2½ cups of water and bring to a boil. Reduce heat to low, cover, and simmer for 15 minutes, stirring occasionally.

3. Meanwhile, in a skillet heat 2 tablespoons oil over medium heat. Add the parsley and mint, and fry for 10 to 15 minutes, stirring occasionally, until the aroma rises from the skillet.

4. Add the parsley and mint mixture, saffron water, tomato paste, and lime juice to the chicken. Bring to a boil, reduce the heat, cover, and simmer 10 minutes.

5. Preheat the oven to 350°F. Transfer the *khoresh* to a deep ovenproof casserole. Arrange the rhubarb on the top and cover the casserole with aluminum foil. Pierce several holes in the foil and place the casserole dish in the oven. Bake for 45 to 50 minutes or until the rhubarb is tender. Remember, rhubarb is fragile: The pieces must be cooked, but not to the point that they are falling apart.

6. Adjust seasoning. If the *khoresh* is too sour, add 1 tablespoon sugar. If the rhubarb needs more cooking, continue until it is soft.

7. Serve hot with saffron steamed rice (*chelow*, pages 89-90). NUSH-E JAN!

Butternut Squash Khoresh

Khoresh-e kadu halvai-o alu

SERVINGS: *4*
PREP TIME: *35 min.*
COOKING TIME: *1½ hours*

5 tablespoons vegetable oil, butter, or ghee*
2 small onions, peeled and thinly sliced
1 pound skinless, boneless chicken or meat (lamb, veal, beef), cut into thin strips
1 teaspoon salt
½ teaspoon freshly ground black pepper
1 teaspoon ground cinnamon
1½ cups pitted prunes or dried golden plums*
2 pounds butternut squash
4 tablespoons sugar
¼ cup fresh lime juice
¼ teaspoon ground saffron threads,* dissolved in 1 tablespoon hot water (optional)

1. In a medium pot, heat 3 tablespoons oil over medium heat. Add the onions and stir-fry 5 minutes, until translucent. Add the chicken and fry for 15 minutes longer, stirring occasionally, until golden brown. Add the salt, pepper, cinnamon, prunes, and 2½ cups water and bring to a boil. Reduce the heat to low, cover, and simmer for 20 minutes, stirring occasionally.

2. Meanwhile, peel the squash and cut it into 2-inch cubes. In a large skillet, heat 2 tablespoons oil over medium heat. Add the squash and stir-fry for 10 minutes, until all sides are golden brown.

3. Add the sugar, lime juice, saffron water, and butternut squash cubes to the chicken. Cover and simmer for 40 minutes over low heat.

4. Taste the *khoresh* and adjust the seasoning for salt and lime juice. In a deep, ovenproof casserole, carefully arrange first the butternut squash, then the chicken. Spoon in the broth. Cover and keep warm until ready to serve.

5. Serve hot with saffron steamed rice (*chelow*, pages 89-90). NUSH-E JAN!

Orange Khoresh

Khoresh-e porteqal

SERVINGS: *4*
PREP TIME: *30 min.*
COOKING TIME: *1 hour*

3 tablespoons vegetable oil, butter, or ghee*
2 small onions, peeled and thinly sliced
1 pound skinless, boneless chicken, or duck breast, or meat (lamb, veal, beef), cut into thin strips
2 large carrots (about ½ pound), peeled and cut into thin strips
2 tablespoons candied orange peel*
1 tablespoon flour
½ teaspoon Persian spice mix (*advieh*)*
1 teaspoon salt
½ teaspoon freshly ground black pepper
2½ cups fresh orange juice
2 tablespoons red wine vinegar
¼ cup fresh lime juice
½ cup sugar
¼ teaspoon ground saffron threads,* dissolved in 1 tablespoon hot water
4 large navel oranges, segmented, with white membrane removed

GARNISH
1 teaspoon slivered or chopped unsalted pistachios
1 teaspoon slivered almonds, toasted*

1. In medium pot heat the oil over medium heat. Add the onions and stir-fry 5 minutes, until translucent. Add the chicken and fry 15 minutes, stirring occasionally, or until golden brown. Add the carrots and orange peel and stir-fry 1 minute longer. Sprinkle in 1 tablespoon flour and stir-fry for a few seconds longer.

2. Add the *advieh*, salt, and pepper. Pour in the orange juice and bring to a boil. Reduce the heat to low, cover, and simmer for 35 minutes.

3. Meanwhile, combine the vinegar, lime juice, sugar, and saffron water in a saucepan. Mix well and bring to a boil over medium heat. Remove from heat, gently add the orange segments and set aside to macerate.

4. Check the chicken for tenderness. Adjust the seasoning, adding more sugar or lime juice according to taste.

5. Transfer to a serving dish, and carefully arrange the orange segments with the sauce on top. Cover and place in a warm oven until ready to serve.

6. Just before serving, sprinkle the *khoresh* with slivered pistachios and almonds. Serve hot with saffron steamed rice (*chelow*, pages 89-90). NUSH-E JAN!

Variation: This *khoresh* may be made with chicken legs, as shown here. If you use them, increase the cooking time in Step 2 to 55 minutes.

Peach Khoresh
Khoresh-e hulu

SERVINGS: *4*
PREP TIME: *30 min.*
COOKING TIME: *1¼ hours*

❧

4 tablespoons vegetable
  oil, butter, or ghee*
2 small onions, peeled
  and thinly sliced
1 pound skinless,
  boneless chicken leg,
  or duck breast, or meat
  (lamb, veal, beef), cut
  into thin strips
1 teaspoon salt
¼ teaspoon freshly
  ground black pepper
½ teaspoon Persian
  spice mix (*advieh*)*
5 firm peaches
½ cup fresh lime juice
½ cup sugar
¼ teaspoon ground
  saffron threads,*
  dissolved in 1
  tablespoon hot water
  (optional)
1 tablespoon fresh
  chopped parsley

It is thought that peaches came from Persia, and their name in most languages derives from the Latin persicum malum, *or "Persian apple." Actually, it is now fairly certain that peaches came to Persia from China but were then introduced to the West from Persia.*

1. In a medium pot, heat 2 tablespoons oil over medium heat. Add the onions and stir-fry 5 minutes, until translucent. Add the chicken and fry 20 minutes, stirring occasionally, until golden brown. Add the salt, pepper, and *advieh*.

2. Pour in 1½ cups of water and bring to a boil. Reduce the heat to low, cover, and simmer for 30 minutes, stirring occasionally.

3. Wash the peaches well to remove fuzz. Remove the pits and cut the peaches into ½-inch wedges. In a large skillet, heat 2 tablespoons oil over medium heat and sauté the peaches carefully for a minute. Add the peaches to the pot.

4. Mix together the lime juice, sugar, and saffron water and stir this mixture into the pot. Cover and simmer 10 to 15 minutes longer over low heat.

5. Check to see whether the chicken and peaches are tender. Taste the *khoresh*: It should taste sweet and sour. Adjust seasonings, adding sugar or lime juice if necessary. Sprinkle with the parsley, cover and keep warm until ready to serve.

6. Serve hot with saffron steamed rice (*chelow*, pages 89-90). NUSH-E JAN!

Variation: 2 cups sliced dried peaches may be substituted for fresh peaches in Step 3.

Apple Khoresh

Khoresh-e sib

SERVINGS: *4*
PREP TIME: *20 min.*
COOKING TIME: *1¼ hours*

❧

4 tablespoons vegetable oil, butter, or ghee*
2 small onions, peeled and thinly sliced
1 pound skinless, boneless chicken leg, or duck breast, or meat (lamb, veal, beef), cut into thin strips
1 teaspoon salt
½ teaspoon freshly ground black pepper
½ teaspoon ground cinnamon
1 tablespoon fresh lime juice
3 tablespoons brown sugar
½ teaspoon ground saffron threads,* dissolved in 2 tablespoons hot water
5 tart cooking apples
1 cup pitted, dried tart cherries*

1. In a medium pot, heat 2 tablespoons oil over medium heat. Add the onions and stir-fry 5 minutes, until translucent. Add the chicken and fry for 15 minutes longer, stirring occasionally, until golden brown. Add the salt, pepper, and cinnamon.

2. Add 2½ cups of water, the lime juice, brown sugar, and saffron water and bring to a boil. Cover and simmer for 20 minutes over low heat, stirring occasionally.

3. Meanwhile, peel and core the apples and cut them into wedges. In a large skillet, heat 2 tablespoons oil over medium heat and fry the apples for 10 to 15 minutes, stirring occasionally, until all sides are golden brown.

4. Preheat the oven to 350°F. Transfer the *khoresh* to a deep ovenproof casserole. Arrange the apples and cherries on top. Cover and bake for 30 minutes, until the apples and meat are tender.

5. Taste the *khoresh*: It should taste sweet and sour. Adjust seasonings, adding sugar or lime juice if necessary. Cover and keep warm until ready to serve.

6. Serve hot with saffron steamed rice (*chelow*, pages 89-90). NUSH-E JAN!

Variation: Instead of dried cherries, you may use ⅓ cup yellow split peas as shown here. If you do, cook the split-peas in 2 cups of water for 20 minutes, drain, and add in Step 4.

Desserts

Saffron Rice Pudding

Paradise Custard

Rose Water Rice Pudding

Cardamom Rice Cookies

Chickpea Cookies

Almond Cookies

Saffron Brownies

Honey Almond Brittle

Pomegranate Jelly

Baklava

*D*ESSERTS

The Persians, Herodotus informed his Greek readers in the fifth century BCE, offer an "abundance of dessert, which is set on table a few dishes at a time; this it is which makes them say that 'the Greeks, when they eat, leave off hungry, having nothing worth mention served up to them after the meats; whereas, if they had more put before them, they would not stop eating.'"

In introducing the concept of sweets after meat to his countrymen, Herodotus was right about the Persians in general, although he was reporting on birthday feasts. At these, as at other special celebrations, Iranian cooks like to present a splendid array of desserts. A traditional wedding banquet, for instance, always includes pastries and other confections—made at the bride's house but paid for by the groom's family—to signify the sweetness and happiness to come in the marriage. Among them are some you will find recipes for on the following pages: *nan-e berenji* (cardamom rice cookies, page 148), *nan-e nokhodchi* (chickpea cookies, page 150), *nan-e badami* (almond cookies, page 151), *sohan asali* (honey-almond brittle, page 154), and perhaps best of all, the rich Persian *baqlava* (pages 156-7).

These traditional treats sweeten Iran's ancient seasonal festivals, too, including the summer water festival, held in July; the harvest festival of early October, and the winter feast, once dedicated to Mithra, God of the sun, and still celebrated on the long night of the Winter Solstice. *Halva*, the saffron brownie shown on page 153, is traditional for this last feast: It is considered a warm food and so an antidote to the cold winds of the dark of the year.

The banquet most associated with sweets, however, is *Nowruz*, the ancient festival that marks the spring equinox and the New Year. According to mythology preserved in Iran's national epic, the *Shahnameh*, this was the day that the legendary King

Jamshid—having brought civilization to Iran by teaching the structuring of society; the building of houses, public baths, and palaces; the construction of boats; the fashioning of fine clothes, jewelry, and scent; and the making of weaponry—appeared in the heavens to his people, flying on his jeweled throne. Among Jamshid's many gifts to Iran, the story says, was the introduction of sugar cane. For that reason, the *Nowruz* feast also often includes an arrangement of seven special sweets. These are the almond, chickpea, and cardamom rice cookies, honey almond brittle and *baqlava* also served at weddings, as well as walnut cookies and sugar-coated almonds.

The truth is that, celebrations aside, Persians are quite fond of sweets. Cookies, pastries, and puddings are served not just as dessert but at any time of day. As travellers have often noticed, they are frequently offered to guests who drop in.

As for everyday meals, a favorite Persian dessert remains the seasonal fruit so much admired by that indefatigable reporter Jean Chardin, who was once deeply impressed, not to say overwhelmed, by an Isfahani banquet displaying 50 different varieties. ("France, or Italy, can't afford anything like it.") No doubt these included the 20 varieties of melon Chardin counted; the purple, red, and black grapes, so big, he said, that one was a mouthful; pomegranates and quinces, which in Persia may be eaten raw; apricots, oranges, and the onions of Bactria, large and sweet as apples; and dates, which he called the best fruits of the world, "covered with thick juice like a syrup, which is clammy, and sticks to the fingers, and is more sweet to the taste than virgin-honey."

A much less extravagant offering of fruits makes a happy ending to any dinner, as do the special confections on the following pages. Whatever you choose should be pretty and fragrant—you will notice the generous use of rose petals and rose water—as well as light. Dessert is meant to refresh both the eye and the palate.

Saffron Rice Pudding

Sholeh zard

SERVINGS: *8*
PREP TIME: *5 min.*
COOKING TIME: *1¾ hours plus ½ hour refrigeration*

1 cup short grain rice
10 cups water
3½ cups sugar
¼ cup unsalted butter
  or corn oil
½ cup slivered almonds
½ teaspoon ground
  saffron threads,*
  dissolved in 2
  tablespoons hot water
1 teaspoon ground
  cardamom
½ cup rose water*
2 tablespoons rice
  flour,* dissolved in 2
  cups water

GARNISH
2 teaspoons ground
  cinnamon
2 teaspoons slivered
  almonds
2 teaspoons slivered or
  chopped unsalted
  pistachios

This easy-to-make, high-calorie dish is often distributed to the homeless and poor as alms during religious ceremonies. Also, if Iranians make a wish that comes true, they often make sholeh zard *and give it away in thanks.*

1. Pick over and wash the rice.

2. Combine the rice with 8 cups of water in a large pot and bring to a boil, skimming the foam as it rises. Cover and simmer for 35 minutes over medium heat until the rice is quite soft.

3. Add the sugar and 2 more cups of warm water and cook for 25 minutes longer, stirring occasionally.

4. Add the butter, almonds, saffron water, cardamom, and rose water and mix well. Cover and simmer over low heat for 20 minutes.

5. Add the dissolved rice flour and cook uncovered over low heat for another 20 minutes or until the mixture has thickened to a pudding.

6. Spoon the pudding into individual serving dishes or a large bowl. Decorate with cinnamon, almonds, and pistachios.

7. Chill the pudding in the refrigerator for at least ½ hour and serve it cold. *NUSH-E JAN!*

Paradise Custard

Yakh dar behesht

SERVINGS: 6
PREP TIME: *10 min.*
COOKING TIME: *15 min.*
plus ½ hour refrigeration

¾ cup cornstarch or rice starch*

4 cups milk

1 cup sugar

Seeds of 10 cardamom pods*

¼ cup rose water*

⅓ cup slivered unsalted almonds, toasted* or 1 teaspoon ground pistachios for garnish

1. In a saucepan, dissolve the cornstarch in the milk and add the sugar.

2. Cook over medium heat for 5 to 10 minutes, stirring constantly, until the mixture has thickened.

3. Add the cardamom seeds and rose water. Stirring constantly with a wire whisk to prevent sticking and lumping, cook for a few minutes longer until the mixture reaches the consistency of a pudding. Remove the saucepan from the heat.

4. Transfer the custard to a serving dish. Garnish with toasted almonds or ground pistachios.

5. Chill the custard in the refrigerator for at least ½ hour and serve it cold. NUSH-E JAN!

Rose Water Rice Pudding

Shir berenj

SERVINGS: *6*
PREP TIME: *5 min.*
COOKING TIME: *1½ hours plus ½ hour refrigeration*

½ cup short-grain rice
2 cups water
¼ teaspoon salt
3 cups milk
½ cup half-and-half or
  cream
¼ cup rose water*
1 teaspoon ground
  cardamom
Grape molasses or
  syrup*

Rice pudding is a common dessert throughout the world; the rose water and cardamom is what distinguishes the Persian version.

1. Pick over and wash the rice.

2. Combine the rice in a saucepan with 2 cups of water and ¼ teaspoon salt. Bring to a boil and reduce the heat. Cover and simmer over medium heat for 20 minutes, or until the rice is tender.

3. Add the milk and half-and-half. Bring to a boil and reduce the heat to low. Cover and cook for about 55 minutes, or until the mixture has thickened to a pudding consistency.

4. Add the rose water and cardamom and cook over low heat for 10 minutes longer.

5. Remove the pudding from the heat. Spoon it into a serving bowl or individual bowls and chill in the refrigerator for at least ½ hour. Serve with grape molasses or syrup,* sugar, jam, raisins, nuts, or honey. NUSH-E JAN!

Cardamom Rice Cookies
Nan-e berenji

SERVINGS: *36 cookies*
PREP TIME: *20 min. plus 30 min. cooling time*
COOKING TIME: *10–15 min. plus 15 min. cooling time*

FOR SYRUP
1½ cups sugar
½ cup water
¼ tablespoon rose
  water*

FOR BATTER
3 egg yolks
1 tablespoon sugar
1 cup clarified butter or
  ghee*
½ cup corn oil
1½ teaspoons ground
  cardamom
3 cups rice flour
2 tablespoons poppy
  seeds

1. Combine the sugar and water in a pot. Bring to a boil and simmer for 4 minutes, being careful not to let the mixture boil over. Remove from the heat, add the rose water, and set aside to cool. This syrup should be room temperature and not too thick. Set aside ¾ cup and bottle the remainder for future use.

2. In a warm mixing bowl, combine the egg yolks with 1 tablespoon sugar and beat well, until creamy.

3. In another mixing bowl, combine the clarified butter, oil, cardamom, and rice flour. Mix well for a few minutes then add the egg yolk mixture and mix a few seconds. Add the ¾ cup syrup from Step 1 and knead well for a few seconds, or until the dough no longer sticks to your hands. This will create a snow-white dough. Allow the dough to cool for 30 minutes at room temperature.

4. Preheat the oven to 350°F. Line a cookie sheet with parchment.

5. Take a spoonful of dough, roll it into a ball the size of a hazelnut, flatten it slightly, and place it on the cookie sheet. Repeat, leaving 2½ inches between each ball. With a fork or the edge of a cookie cutter, draw geometric patterns on the cookies and sprinkle them with poppy seeds. You may also use a cookie press (readily available in most cookware stores) to stamp a design in the dough.

6. Place the cookie sheet in the center of the preheated oven and bake the cookies 10 to 15 minutes. Keep in mind that the cookies should be white when they are done.

7. Remove the cookies from the oven and cool. Lift the cookies off the baking paper carefully: They crumble very easily.

8. Arrange the cookies in a pyramid on a footed cake dish. NUSH-E JAN!

Chickpea Cookies

Nan-e nokhodchi

SERVINGS: *36 cookies*
PREP TIME: *30 min. plus 2 hours' setting time*
COOKING TIME: *10–15 min. plus 15 min. refrigeration*

½ cup clarified butter or ghee*
½ cup corn oil
1½ cup confectioners' sugar
2 tablespoons ground cardamom
4½ cups sifted chickpea flour*
2 tablespoons unsalted, slivered or chopped pistachios for garnish

1. In a mixing bowl, combine the clarified butter, oil, sugar, and cardamom, and mix well until creamy. Gradually add the chickpea flour, stirring constantly to produce a dough. Knead well for 10 minutes, until the dough no longer sticks to your hands. Cover and set aside for 2 hours at room temperature.

2. Place a piece of parchment paper on the counter, place the dough in the center, then place another piece of parchment paper on top. Roll the dough out to a ½-inch thickness and chill for at least 15 minutes.

3. Preheat the oven to 300°F. Line a cookie sheet with parchment paper.

4. Remove the dough from the refrigerator, place on a flat surface and cut out cookies with a tiny cloverleaf cookie cutter. Garnish each cookie with pistachios. Place the cookies on the sheet, leaving 1 inch between pieces to allow them to spread.

5. Place the cookie sheet in the center of the oven and bake the cookies 10 to 15 minutes, until slightly golden.

6. Remove the cookies from the oven and cool. Lift the cookies off the baking paper carefully: They crumble very easily.

7. Arrange the cookies in a pyramid on a platter. NUSH-E JAN!

Almond Cookies

Nan-e badami

SERVINGS: *20 cookies*
PREP TIME: *40 min.*
COOKING TIME: *10–20 min.*

1 pound blanched almonds*
5 egg whites
1½ cups confectioners' sugar
½ teaspoon ground cardamom or 2 tablespoons rose water*
2 tablespoons unsalted, slivered or chopped pistachios or slivered almonds, toasted* for garnish

1. In a food processor, grind the blanched almonds to powder.

2. In a mixing bowl, beat the egg whites until foamy. Slowly mix in the sugar, almond powder, and cardamom. Gently mix until a dough is formed.

3. Preheat the oven to 350°F. Line a cookie sheet with parchment paper.

4. Scoop out a full tablespoon of the dough and place it on the lined cookie sheet. Repeat, leaving 2½ inches between each piece for expansion. Garnish each piece with a few slivered pistachios or toasted almond slivers.

5. Place the cookie sheet in the center of the oven and bake for 10 to 20 minutes, until the cookies are light gold.

6. Remove the cookies from the oven, cool, and then remove them from the cookie sheet. Keep them in a cookie jar.

7. When ready to serve, arrange in a pyramid on a footed cake dish. *NUSH-E JAN!*

Saffron Brownie

Halva

SERVINGS: *6*
PREP TIME: *10 min.*
COOKING TIME: *30 min. plus 30 min. refrigeration*

FOR SYRUP
- 1 cup water
- 1 cup sugar
- 1 teaspoon ground saffron threads,* dissolved in ¼ cup hot water
- ¼ cup rose water*
- ½ teaspoon ground cardamom

FOR DOUGH
- 2 cups sifted all-purpose flour
- 1½ cups melted unsalted butter, corn oil, or ghee*

FOR GARNISH
- 4 tablespoons chopped unsalted pistachios

Because it is a high-calorie dish, Persian halva *was traditionally eaten with bread by the poor as the main meal. In Persian* halva *means "soft and sweet" in the sense of being pliable, for example: "He's so smitten, he's* halva *in her hands." If kept cold,* halva *is actually quite firm. As it warms up it softens somewhat, but if made properly, should not crumble. My sons like to take pieces wrapped in foil along with them on hikes, as homemade "energy bars."*

1. Bring the water and sugar to a boil in a saucepan. Remove from heat and add the saffron water, rose water, and ground cardamom. Mix the syrup well and set aside.

2. In a large, deep skillet, toast the flour for about 10 minutes over medium heat, stirring constantly with a wooden spoon. Add the melted butter and fry, mixing constantly with a wooden spoon for 7 to 15 minutes, until golden brown. (This stage is very important: Be careful that the flour is not over- or undercooked). Remove the skillet from the heat.

3. Gradually blend the syrup into the hot flour-and-butter mixture, stirring quickly and constantly with a wooden spoon for about 5 minutes. To make a thick, smooth paste, transfer to a food processor and mix well for 5 minutes. If the paste does not set, return it to the pan, place it over high heat again, and stir constantly until the mixture is thick and smooth.

4. Spoon the paste onto a flat plate or pie dish and pack it firmly with a spoon. Decorate by making geometric patterns with a spoon and garnish with pistachios.

5. Cover and chill the saffron brownie in the refrigerator for 2 hours. Cut it into small pieces and serve cold as a main dish with *lavash* bread or alone as a dessert. *NUSH-E JAN!*

Variation: You can use whole wheat flour instead of white flour. If you do, add ¼ cup more water and ¼ cup more sugar to the syrup.

Variation: You may also make individual portions of *halva*, as shown to the right. To do so, spread the paste on a flat surface, then stamp out shapes with cookie cutters. Place these in petit-four cases, which may be purchased at paper or party stores.

Honey Almond Brittle

Sohan asali

SERVINGS: *25 pieces*
PREP TIME: *15 min.*
COOKING TIME: *10 min.*
plus 10 min. cooling time

1 cup sugar
3 tablespoons honey
4 tablespoons corn oil
1½ cups slivered,
    blanched almonds*
¼ teaspoon ground
    saffron threads,*
    dissolved in 2
    tablespoons of rose
    water*
4 tablespoons unsalted,
    slivered or chopped
    pistachios for garnish

1. Place a mixing bowl of ice water next to the stove.

2. In a heavy saucepan melt the sugar and honey with the oil over medium heat for 5 minutes, stirring occasionally.

3. Add the slivered almonds to the mixture. Cook, stirring occasionally, for 2 to 3 minutes, until the mixture is firm and golden.

4. Add the saffron-rose water mixture and, stirring occasionally with a wooden spoon, cook for another 2 to 4 minutes until the mixture is golden brown. Be careful: It should not be dark brown. Drop a spoonful of the hot almond mixture into the ice water: If it hardens immediately, the mixture is ready. Reduce the heat to very low.

5. Spread a piece of parchment paper on a flat surface. Place teaspoonfuls of the mixture on the paper, leaving 1-inch spaces between them. Garnish immediately with the slivered pistachios.

6. Allow the almond brittle to cool for 10 minutes, then remove from the paper.

7. Arrange on a serving platter. Cover with a sheet of aluminum foil to keep the pieces crisp or keep them in an airtight container or cookie jar. NUSH-E JAN!

Variation: Walnuts or sesame seeds can be substituted for the almonds.

Pomegranate Jelly

Jeleh-ye anar

SERVINGS: *6*
PREP TIME: *10 min.*
COOKING TIME: *5 min.*
plus 8 hours' refrigeration

3 tablespoons
    unflavored gelatin or
    4 tablespoons
    cornstarch
5 cups fresh
    pomegranate juice*
2 tablespoons fresh lime
    juice
2 tablespoons sugar (if
    pomegranate juice is
    too sour)
Seeds of 4 fresh
    pomegranates*

1. In a large bowl, mix the unflavored gelatin in 1 cup of cold pomegranate juice. Let stand for 1 minute.

2. In a saucepan, warm the lime juice and remaining pomegranate juice.

3. Add the gelatin mixture to the saucepan. Stir constantly for 5 minutes, until the gelatin is completely dissolved.

4. Taste. If the mixture is too sour, add sugar to taste. Pour the mixture into a mold or a bowl. Let it cool.

5. Sprinkle the pomegranate seeds on top of the mixture. Chill in the refrigerator until firm.

6. Serve pomegranate jelly alone or with yogurt or ice cream. NUSH-E JAN!

Variation: This jelly can be equally well made with tart cherries* or rhubarb. Replace the pomegranate juice and seeds with tart cherry juice and tart cherries or with rhubarb juice.*

Baklava

Baqlava

SERVINGS: *1 full sheet*
PREP TIME: *35 min. plus 30 min. to rest*
COOKING TIME: *35 min. plus 24 hours' to rest*

FOR SYRUP
2½ cups sugar
1½ cups water
½ cup rose water*
1 tablespoon fresh
  lemon juice

FOR DOUGH
¼ cup low-fat milk, 2%
  milk fat
½ cup corn oil
1 tablespoon cooled
  syrup (above)
¼ cup rose water*
1 egg
2½ cups sifted all-
  purpose flour

FOR FILLING
2 pounds blanched
  almonds, ground*
2 cups sugar
2 tablespoons ground
  cardamom

4 tablespoons corn oil
  for baking
2 tablespoons chopped
  or ground unsalted
  pistachios for garnish

This sweet flaky pastry, filled with chopped nuts and topped with sugar syrup, has come to be known and enjoyed worldwide. The origins of the word are probably Persian, either from pokhtan, *meaning "cooking" or from* balg, *meaning "leaf." Persian* baqlava *uses a combination of chopped almonds and pistachios spiced with cardamom and a rose water-scented syrup. It is a subtle, delicate blend of flavors, quite different from the taste of other Middle Eastern versions. While many Persians still make the thin dough at home, frozen, ready-to-use phyllo pastry is an acceptable alternative.*

1. Prepare the syrup by combining the sugar and water in a saucepan. Bring to a boil, add the rose water and lemon juice, and immediately remove from heat to prevent overboiling.

2. For the dough, combine the milk, corn oil, 1 tablespoon of the syrup, rose water, and egg in a food processor or dough maker. Add the flour and mix well for 5 to 10 minutes to form a dough that is elastic and does not stick to your hands. Divide the dough into 2 balls of equal size and place in a bowl. Cover with a clean towel and let rest for 30 minutes.

3. For the filling, finely grind the almonds, sugar, and cardamom together in a food processor. (There may be too much to fit in your food processor, in which case grind in two batches). Set aside.

4. When the dough has rested, grease a 17-by-11-by-1-inch baking sheet with 2 tablespoons oil and preheat the oven to 350°F.

5. Prepare a large, wide area for rolling out the dough. Cover the surface with a dusting of flour. Remove 1 ball of dough from the bowl and roll out into a very thin rectangular layer with a thin wooden rolling pin. Roll dough from the center to the outside edge in all directions, giving it a quarter turn occasionally for an even thickness. The finished dough should be thinner than a pie crust and large enough to overlap the cookie sheet.

6. Roll the thin layer of dough around the wooden rolling pin. Place it on the greased cookie sheet and unroll the dough until it covers the whole cookie sheet. Do not cut off the excess dough; let the dough hang over the edge of the cookie sheet 1 inch on all sides.

7. Evenly sprinkle all the almond-filling mixture on top of the dough. Spread, smooth, and press the mixture onto the dough with your hand.

8. Roll the second ball of dough out into a very thin rectangular layer as in Step 5. Roll the layer around the rolling pin, place on top of the filling mixture in the cookie sheet, and unroll the dough to cover the mixture, allowing it to hang over all sides like the bottom layer. Press down on the dough evenly with your hands all over the dough's surface.

9. Using a sharp knife, trace a cross-hatching of diamond shapes over the surface of the dough. Each diamond should be about 1 inch wide.

10. Fold the overhanging edges of the top layer of dough under the edges

of the bottom layer. Press and pinch them together, forming a rim around the baklava as you would form a rim to seal a pie.

11. With a sharp knife, pressing and steadying the dough with one hand, cut through the incised diamond pattern on the top of the dough. Then paint the dough with 2 tablespoons of corn oil and transfer the baking sheet to the middle level of the preheated oven.

12. Bake for 30 to 35 minutes, until the baklava looks pink. Then remove the pan from the oven and pour 1 cup of the syrup evenly over the top of the baklava.

13. Decorate the baklava with chopped or ground pistachios. Cover it tightly with aluminum foil and let stand for 24 hours.

14. Serve from the baking pan or, using a sharp knife, lift out the diamond pieces and arrange them on a serving dish. *NUSH-E JAN!*

Note: Baklava will keep, covered, in the refrigerator for 3 weeks and in the freezer up to 3 months. When serving it later, you may freshen it by warming ½ cup of syrup and pouring it evenly over the top of the pastry.

Variation: The dough can be divided into three layers. Between them you can place 1 pound of unsalted pistachios, blanched and ground with 1 cup sugar and teaspoon cardamom; and another layer made of 1 pound of almonds, blanched and ground with 1 cup sugar and 1 teaspoon cardamom. You can also substitute honey for the syrup.

Variation: If you wish to make baklava with frozen phyllo pastry, make sure you purchase the kind intended for baklava use. Defrost the pastry, unopened, in the refrigerator. Then let it sit, still unopened, at room temperature for several hours. Open the package and unfold the pastry onto a dry towel. Immediately cover it with another moist towel to prevent the pastry from drying out. To form baklava, grease a 12-by-9-by-2-inch baking sheet. Place one sheet of phyllo on it. Brush the pastry with oil and lay a second sheet of phyllo over it. Repeat with a third, fourth, and fifth sheet and then spread the almond filling from Step 2 over the pastry. Cover with five oiled sheets of phyllo, and continue from Step 9, above.

Appendices

A Dictionary of Persian Cooking

Cooking Measurements

Persian Groceries & Restaurants

Index

A DICTIONARY OF PERSIAN COOKING

ALMOND, SWEET (*BADAM*)

Iran is the center from which almonds spread, on the one hand to Europe and on the other to Tibet and China. Almonds have long been favored by Persian cooks: Fresh ripe and unripe almonds in their soft shells, sprinkled with salt, make popular snacks; the ripe nuts also provide a delicate flavoring for pastries and a thickener for *khoresh*es.

For freshness, buy shelled, unblanched nuts. To blanch, drop the almonds into boiling water, boil for 1 minute, drain, and slip off the loosened skins. Then spread the nuts on a baking sheet and dry them for 5 minutes in a 350°F oven. Blanched almonds may be slivered or ground to powder in a food processor. Store whole or ground blanched almonds in airtight containers in the freezer. To roast, see NUTS, ROASTING; to toast, see NUTS, TOASTING.

ANGELICA (*GOL-PAR*)

This giant member of the parsley family is named after angels both in English and Persian: The Persian word is a compound of *gol*, or "flower," and *pari*, or "angel." According to folklore, the English name derives from the fact that angelica is best harvested around September 29, the Feast of St. Michael and All Angels. The Persian term honors the herb as a panacea. Its seeds, alone or burned with wild rue, defend against the evil eye; powdered seeds aid digestion; and the pungent roots and leaves are brewed for tea.

Western cooks know angelica in the form of decorative candied leaves. Persian cooks use the seeds and powder as souring agents for dishes containing pomegranates, and in soups and stews. Both seeds and powder are sold at Persian groceries.

BARBERRIES (*ZERESHK*)

These are the tart red fruit, high in malic and citric acids, of a bush now only used for ornamental hedges in the West. In Iranian folklore, the thorny wild bushes are said to be the refuge of a gray partridge (white during a certain part of the season), whose wings are stained red by the fruit.

Barberries, usually too sour to be eaten raw (though as children we often enjoyed them as a tart snack), are little appreciated in the West: In Europe, they were once pickled or made into syrups, jam, or wine and medieval Western recipes mention barberries. However, since the discovery that the barberry bush harbored the spores of a wheat blight, their planting has been prohibited in many areas in the West. In Iran, on the other hand, the berries' tart taste and bright, jewel-like color make the fruit a favorite for flavoring and seasoning. Fresh barberry juice (often sold by street vendors in Iran) is said to lower blood pressure and cleanse the system.

The berries usually are dried and stored, and you will find them at Persian groceries. Be sure to choose red ones: Dark berries may be elderly leftovers from earlier seasons.

Dried berries must be cleansed of sand before cooking. Stem the fruit, place it in a colander, and partly immerse the colander in cold water. Let it rest for 20 minutes, while the sand sinks to the bottom of the colander. Then remove it from the water, run fresh cold water over the berries, and drain them. Fresh barberries, if you should find them, need only be stemmed and rinsed.

BREADS, PERSIAN (*NAN*)

Among various Persian breads available in this country is *nan-e sangak*, or stone bread, a flat, rectangular loaf 3 feet long, 18 inches wide, and 1 inch thick. It is baked over hot stones—hence the name—and served warm. *Nan-e barbari*, a flat, oval loaf about 2 inches thick, is eaten very fresh and warm, usually for breakfast. *Nan-e lavash*, the oldest known Middle Eastern bread, is a light, crusty oval or disk about 2 feet wide. In Iranian villages it once was baked every few months in a *tanour*, or bread oven, then wrapped in a clean cloth and used as needed, for it keeps very well. Nowadays it is fresh baked every afternoon. *Nan-e sangak* is sold at Persian groceries; *nan-e barbari* and *nan-e lavash* are sold at both Persian groceries and supermarkets. *Nan-e sangak* and *nan-e barbari* should be warmed for two minutes on the center rack of a preheated 400°F oven. *Nan-e lavash* needs only a minute for perfect consistency.

BROTH (*GUSHTABEH*)

Making either chicken or beef broth is a simple matter of simmering meat with aromatic vegetables in water and straining and defatting the flavored liquid that results:

> 4-5 pounds chicken parts (skinless drumsticks, breast bones, wings, backs, or scraps), or raw beef or veal bones
> 1 large onion, peeled and sliced
> 2 cloves garlic, whole
> 2 carrots, chopped
> 2 celery stalks, chopped
> 2 leeks, chopped
> 1 parsnip, chopped

1. Bundle the herbs in cheesecloth and tie shut.
2. Combine all ingredients in a large pot. Cover with 8 cups water and bring to a boil, skimming off the froth as it rises.
3. Reduce heat, cover, and simmer for 2 hours over low heat.
4. Strain broth through a sieve and discard the solids. Allow to cool.
5. Store broth in a lidded jar, skim excess fat from top, cover and refrigerate. Use as needed.

Broth freezes beautifully, and many cooks keep a frozen supply on hand. Lacking frozen broth, you may substitute canned beef or chicken broth. Broth made from bouillon cubes, however, is both underflavored and oversalted. Do not use it.

BUTTER, CLARIFIED
See GHEE.

CARDAMOM (*HEL*)

This widely available, highly flavored spice, a member of the ginger family, is native to India; travelling via caravan routes, it became a favorite in Iran, Greece, and Rome by classical times.

Cardamom is sold as green, white, or black pods. For Persian cookery, white pods are the first choice, green the second. Black pods have a distinctive smoky flavor best avoided. Within the pods are tiny, black, fragrant seeds, known in Iran as "seeds of Paradise." Iranians sometimes suck on the whole pods to sweeten the breath, especially after eating garlic.

In cookery, whole pods serve as decoration for some dishes, and the seeds, extracted with the tip of a knife, flavor rice and sweets. For recipes specifying ground cardamom, Iranians grind the whole spice, pod and all. Commercial ground cardamom is an acceptable substitute.

CAVIAR (*KHAVIAR*)

The unfertilized, processed roe of the sturgeon, this most exotic of appetizers probably takes its name from the Persian term *mahi-e Khayedar*, which means literally "egg-bearing fish." The best caviar comes from the Caspian Sea.

In buying caviar, you will have a basic choice of three varieties. The largest eggs go by the Russian name, *beluga*; medium-sized eggs are called *osetra*, and small eggs *sevruga*. Each has its own distinctive flavor: Tasting will tell you which you like best. Different brands vary in quality, but the test for freshness is always the same: Smell the roe. Fresh caviar, like fresh oysters, smells of the sea but not of fish. While Caspian provincial cookery offers several recipes incorporating caviar, and Russians serve it with chopped onion and egg white, the roe is at its best when presented simply, with buttered toast and a little fresh lime juice.

CHEESE, PERSIAN (*PANIR*)

A soft, white cheese similar to feta, *panir* is made from cow or goat's milk. Any soft, white cheese is a suitable substitute, or you can make your own. The recipe that follows takes about 20 minutes plus 3 hours' draining and setting time, and serves six.

> ½ gallon whole milk
> 1 cup plain yogurt
> 2 tablespoons salt (optional)
> ¼ cup fresh lime juice
> ½ teaspoon salt
> 1 tablespoon plain yogurt

1. Bring the milk to a boil in a large, nonreactive pot set over low heat. Stir in the cup of yogurt, optional salt, and lime juice, and simmer gently for 3 to 5 minutes, until the mixture turns yellow. Immediately pour it through a strainer lined with three layers of cheesecloth and set in a large container. Let the mixture drain into the container for several minutes.

Strain the drained liquid and reserve it.

2. Pull the ends of the cheesecloth together over the mixture to enclose it, and return the bundle to the center of the strainer. Place a heavy weight on the bundle, and allow it to drain for 2 hours. Remove the weight, place the bundle in a bowl, and refrigerate for 1 hour to set.

3. Unwrap the cheese and place it in a clean jar. Fill the jar with the reserved strained liquid, add ¼ teaspoon salt and 1 tablespoon yogurt, and refrigerate until ready to serve.

CHERRIES, TART OR SOUR (*ALBALU*)

Tart cherries are available fresh in the summer and dried, canned, or frozen all year round in supermarkets or Persian groceries. The following are the ways each type can be prepared for inclusion in Rice with Tart Cherries (page 108). These recipes require 5 minutes' preparation, up to 35 minutes' cooking, and produce enough cherries and syrup for a recipe serving 6 people.

For fresh tart cherries: Use 4 pounds of fresh tart cherries. Rinse them in cold water, remove the stems and pit the cherries over a stainless steel pot (you don't want to lose any of the juice). Add 1½ cups of sugar and cook over medium heat for 35 minutes. Drain, saving the cherries and the syrup separately for later use as instructed in the recipe.

For frozen pitted sour cherries: Combine 2 pounds of frozen pitted sour cherries with 1 cup of sugar, bring to a boil over medium heat, and cook for 35 minutes. Drain, saving the cherries and the syrup separately for later use as instructed in the recipe.

For tart, sour, or morello cherries in light syrup: Use three 1½-pound jars. Drain the cherries, combine them with 1 cup of sugar in a saucepan, and boil over medium heat for 35 minutes. Drain, saving the cherries and the syrup separately for later use as instructed in the recipe.

For dried tart or sour cherries: In a heavy pot, combine 4 cups of cherries with 1 cup of sugar and 2 cups of water. Bring to a boil over medium heat, cook for 35 minutes, and stir in 2 tablespoons of fresh lime juice. Drain, saving the cherries and the syrup separately for later use as instructed in the recipe.

CHICKPEA FLOUR (*ARD-E NOKHODCHI*)

Flour is one of the many products made from the chickpea, or garbanzo bean. It is sold at specialty and Iranian groceries. For the finest flavor, buy roasted chickpea flour.

CILANTRO
See CORIANDER.

CINNAMON (*DARCHIN*)

This spice, made from the bark of various Asian evergreen trees, is one of the oldest: It was first recorded in China in 2500 BCE. It is widely available as sticks (curled pieces of branch bark), chunks (pieces from more intense-tasting bark low on the tree), and ground spice, which is the kind used in Iranian cookery. Chinese and Vietnamese cassia cinnamon are familiar varieties, sweet and aromatic. "True" cinnamon, from cinnamon trees in Ceylon, is milder, with more of a citrus scent. Either may be used in Iranian cookery. Just be sure the spice is fresh: Even stored in tightly sealed jars, cinnamon deteriorates after a few months.

CORIANDER (*GISHNIZ*)

Coriander is native to Iran. It is sold in two quite different forms, both easy to find. Fresh leaves are known in America as cilantro, Chinese parsley, or Mexican parsley and have an intense, musky taste. They need only be rinsed and stemmed before use. Coriander seeds, which look like pale peppercorns, have a concentrated, fiery flavor. They are sold ground for use in cooking, but whole seeds can also be ground in a spice mill or small coffee grinder used exclusively for spices.

CUMIN (*ZIREH*)

Cumin is the dried seed of a plant in the parsley family. It is native to Iran, from where it was introduced to China in the second century. Pungent, hot, and rather bitter, a little adds complexity to many dishes. Iranian cumin, highest in essential oils and therefore in flavor, is not currently available in the West, but Indian cumin is an acceptable substitute.

CURRY POWDER (*KARI*)

Commercial curry powder comes in a range of flavors and intensities from sweet to hot. All are mixtures of roasted, ground spices, generally including turmeric (the source of the yellow color), coriander, cumin, fenugreek, ginger, nutmeg, fennel, cinnamon, cardamom, and various peppers. Sweeter—i.e. milder—curry powder is best for Iranian dishes.

DATES (*KHORMA*)

The date palm has been cherished for millennia in Iran and western Asia for its succulent fruit, which is said to have 360 uses: Among the products made from it have been flour, wine, soft drinks, syrup (dates are 50 percent sugar), and medicine for chest and other ailments. In addition, the pits can be ground to make a coffee substitute, and the sap fermented to make a toddy.

For eating and cooking, you will find three kinds of date. Soft dates, harvested when unripe, are a delicious fruit just for eating; you will find them in specialty groceries. Semi-dry dates, from firmer varieties, are more syrupy and intense in flavor; the most widely sold U.S. variety is Deglet Noor. Dry dates are sun-dried on the trees, and are very firm and sugary. These hold their shape best in cooked dishes. Both are sold in supermarkets.

EGGPLANT (*BADEMJAN*)

As many as 40 varieties of eggplant are sold in supermarkets. They range from the familiar long purple eggplant to Japanese and pale lavender Chinese species, narrow and as long as 10 inches. Whichever you choose, make sure the vegetable is firm and the skin smooth and shiny.

Chinese eggplants require no particular preparation before cooking. The flesh of the long purple, however, should be steeped before stewing, baking, or frying to draw out its excess, sometimes bitter, juices. This is the best method: Peel the eggplants, slice them according to your recipe, place them in a colander in the sink, and sprinkle them with salt, allowing 1 tablespoon of salt per 2 pounds of eggplant. Let the slices steep for 20 minutes, rinse them with cold water, and pat them dry.

FAVA BEANS (*BAQALI*)

Also known as broad beans, fava beans are sold in the pod during the summer at specialty groceries and some supermarkets. Shelled beans are also available frozen. When shopping for fresh beans, choose those with tightly closed, bulging, dark-green pods. If stored in perforated plastic bags, they will keep for one or two days in the refrigerator.

To shell a bean, press down on the seam near the stem and split the seam with your thumbnail to pop out the beans. Each bean is covered with a protective membrane; split it with your thumbnail and pull it off in one piece.

FENUGREEK (*SHANBALILEH*)

Although its English name—from the Latin *fenum graecum*, or "Greek hay"—refers to a Mediterranean origin, this herb actually is native to Iran, from where it was introduced to the classical world in antiquity and to China in the second century.

Fenugreek seeds are very hard and therefore difficult to pulverize, so this is one herb that is generally sold ground. Some nomadic tribes in Iran soak the seeds to make a jelly, which is said to be good for the digestion. The rather bitter fresh leaves are sometimes baked whole in bread and are an indispensable ingredient in Fresh Herb Khoresh (page 118).

GARLIC, SWEET FRESH (*SEER-E TAZEH*)

This vegetable, which looks like large spring onions and has only the mildest garlic taste, is sold in specialty groceries and some supermarkets in the spring. If it is not available, use regular garlic.

GHEE (*ROGHAN-E KAREH*)

A staple in Persian kitchens, ghee is clarified butter, which gives a delicious nutty taste to rice and pastries and has a higher scorching point than regular butter. It is sold in health-food stores and Persian groceries, but it is easy to make at home: Melt 1 pound of unsalted butter in a saucepan. When it bubbles, cover and simmer over low heat for 15 to 20 minutes, until most of the froth subsides. Let it cool in the pan for 5 minutes. Then strain the liquid through one layer of muslin or three layers of cheesecloth to separate the clear butter fat from the milk solids. Discard the solids and store the ghee (the clear butter fat) in a tightly closed jar in your refrigerator.

GRAPE LEAVES (*BARG-E MO*)
In America, fresh grape leaves are a rarity: Most of the commercial crop is canned. If you should find fresh leaves, choose the smallest and tenderest ones. Snip off the ends and wash thoroughly. Stack the leaves in bundles of 25, veins facing up, and tie them with a string. Blanch each stack in boiling salted water for 2 minutes, allowing ½ cup of salt for 12 cups of water. Drain the leaves in a colander, rinse with cold water, remove the strings and pat the leaves dry. To use canned grape leaves, simply drain the brine, unroll, rinse in cold water, and pat dry.

GRAPE SYRUP, MOLASSES, OR PASTE
(*DUSHAB-E ANGUR*)
This sweet, jam-like paste is available at Persian, Afghan, and Armenian groceries. You can also make your own. The following recipe requires 30 minutes' preparation, 2½ hours' cooking, and makes ½ pint of syrup.

2 cups pure grape juice
¼ cup charcoal powder or 4 charcoal tablets (available in drugstores)
10 pounds seedless grapes
½ teaspoon ground cardamom

1. Mix the grape juice with the charcoal, stirring until the charcoal powder is completely dissolved. Let stand 30 minutes.
2. Meanwhile, wash and stem the grapes. Purée them in a food processor and pour the purée into a nonreactive pot.
3. Gently pour the juice into the grape purée, leaving any sediment behind.
4. Bring the mixture to a boil, reduce the heat to low, and simmer for 2 to 3 hours, stirring frequently to prevent burning, until it thickens.
5. Stir in the cardamom and remove the mixture from the heat. Pour the grape syrup into sterilized canning jars, leaving ¼-inch headspace, put on the lids, and process in a boiling-water bath (canner) for 10 minutes. Store in a cool, dark place.

GRAPES, UNRIPE (*GHUREH*)
These grapes, used as a souring agent in many Iranian dishes, are sold at Persian groceries in various forms: Fresh in season, whole frozen, and canned; as unripe grape juice (*ab-ghureh*), also known as verjuice; and as powdered unripe grapes (*gard-e ghureh*). Although the taste will not be quite the same, you can substitute fresh lime juice for them in recipes: Allow 4 tablespoons of lime juice per 1½ cups of unripe grapes, 1 cup of juice, or 1 teaspoon of powder.

HERBS, DRIED (*SABZI-E KHOSHK*)
If you must use dried herbs, use only one-quarter of the fresh herbs called for, to allow for the greater intensity of the dried product. For the best flavor, soak the dried herbs in a sieve set in a bowl of lukewarm water for 15 minutes, then drain them and proceed with the recipe.

LIMES, PERSIAN (*LIMU*)
The lime variety known as Persian lime has been grown in Iran for many centuries. These limes are widely available fresh. Persian groceries stock dried limes (*limu omani*) from California (which sometimes have seeds) and the dried lime powder (*gard-e limu omani*) made from them. This commercial powder is apt to be bitter, because it contains ground seeds, but it is easy to make your own from dried Persian limes: With a knife, crack open the limes, halve them, and remove any seeds. Then grind the dried limes to powder in a food processor, and store in an airtight jar.

NOODLES, PERSIAN (*RESHTEH*)
Iranian flour noodles are sold dried or toasted and dried at Persian groceries. Lacking Iranian noodles, you may substitute any flat, narrow, dried noodle, such as linguine. To toast noodles yourself, toss them in a hot, ungreased skillet for a few minutes, until they are golden brown, or spread them on a baking sheet and broil them under high heat for 30 seconds.

NUTS, ROASTING
To roast nuts or seeds such as pumpkin seeds for appetizers, combine 1 pound nuts or seeds, 1 cup water, and 1 tablespoon salt in a large skillet set over low heat. Cook, stirring occasionally, until the water evaporates. Then stir constantly until the nuts are dry and brown. Shake the nuts in a colander or sieve to remove excess salt, then spread them on a baking sheet and, if you wish, sprinkle them with saffron water, lime juice, or

spices to your taste. Shake the sheet to distribute the flavorings, and bake the nuts or seeds in a 250°F oven for 1 to 1½ hours, until completely dried. Store in an airtight jar.

NUTS, TOASTING

Heat a large skillet over medium heat and add nuts, but no oil. Cook over medium heat, stirring constantly, until the nuts are golden brown—5 to 10 minutes. Store in an airtight jar.

ONION JUICE

Onion juice for marinades should be made just before use: It turns bitter if left to stand. To make 1 cup of juice, purée 2 large peeled yellow onions in a food processor. Strain the purée through a fine-mesh sieve or food mill into a bowl, pressing to extract all the juice.

ORANGE (PORTEQAL / NARENJ)

Oranges come in two main varieties: Sweet, or eating oranges, including the California and navel oranges found in every supermarket; and the less often available slightly bitter type, known as the Seville, bitter, wild or bigerade orange (narenj). The blossoms of the Seville orange are used in Iran for their perfume and for a wonderful jam, called moraba-ye bahar narenj. In cookery Seville juice and paste impart a fine, astringent taste to many fish dishes.

Bitter or Seville oranges grew wild along the Caspian thousands of years ago. They were taken to China via the Silk Road, and centuries later, a hybridized sweet orange was returned to Iran by Portuguese merchants. The sweet orange reached Europe in the first, tenth, or fifteenth century, according to various sources, and ironically, took its western name from the Persian narenj, or bitter orange, while in Iran, the sweet orange is called porteqal, after the Portuguese merchants who imported it.

The flesh of the Seville orange is too bitter to eat, but its juice is much used in Iranian cookery, and some recipes call for the intensity of Seville orange paste, made from the juice. Lacking Seville orange juice, you may substitute ¼ cup of fresh sweet orange juice plus 2 tablespoons fresh lime juice for every ½ cup of the Seville juice called for in a recipe. For treatments of orange peel and paste, see below.

ORANGE PASTE, SEVILLE (ROB-E NARENJ)

Seville orange paste is sold in Persian groceries. You can also make it at home. This recipe requires 20 Seville oranges, 45 minutes' preparation time and 1½ hours' cooking time, and produces 1 cup of paste.

1. Remove the peel in a 1-inch wide strip around the middle of each orange: This reduces the bitterness. Halve the orange and remove the seeds. Juice each orange, and strain the juice.

2. Pour the juice into a non-reactive pot, bring it to a boil, reduce the heat to medium, and simmer, uncovered, over medium heat for about 1½ hours. As the juice thickens, you will need to stir constantly, to prevent sticking and burning; when it has reduced to a thick, soft paste, remove it from the heat.

3. Store the paste in a tightly closed jar in the refrigerator

ORANGE PEEL, BLANCHED (PUST-E PORTEQAL)

You may use either orange peel or tangerine peel for recipes. In either case, the peel should be blanched to remove the bitterness. To do so, peel the orange (or tangerine) and cut the layers of skin into slivers. Drop the slivers into boiling water and cook over medium heat for 7 to 10 minutes, then drain in a colander and rinse under cold running water. It saves time to blanch a good supply of orange peel: Stored in small 1-cup portions in plastic bags in the freezer, it will keep for several months.

ORANGE PEEL, CANDIED (PUST-E PORTEQAL-E SHIRIN)

Candied peel appears in supermarkets during the winter, but it is easy to make at home. The following recipe takes about 20 minutes' preparation and 45 minutes' cooking, and makes 1 cup of candied peel:

4 oranges
4 cups sugar
2 cups water
4 tablespoons fresh lime juice

1. Wash the oranges, peel them, cut the peel into slivers, and blanch (see above).
2. In a saucepan, combine the blanched peel, the sugar, and the water. Bring to a boil, reduce the heat to medium, and simmer for 20 min-

utes. Add the lime juice and simmer 15 to 20 minutes more.

3. Drain the peel, spread it on parchment paper, and let it dry for a few hours. Then sprinkle with confectioners' sugar if desired and store in a plastic bag in the refrigerator for weeks or in the freezer for months.

PEAS, SPLIT (*LAPEH*)

Yellow split peas, the kind specified in recipes in this book, come in two main varieties, which are interchangeable. Those sold in supermarkets take 20 minutes to cook; however those sold in Persian groceries take at least 40 minutes, and you should adjust recipe cooking times accordingly.

PERSIAN SPICE MIX (*ADVIEH*)

The spice mix called for in Persian recipes is sold at Persian groceries, but it is easy to make at home. This basic recipe takes only a few minutes to make, and produces about ½ cup:

  2 tablespoons dried rose petals
  2 tablespoons ground cinnamon
  2 tablespoons ground cardamom
  1 tablespoon ground cumin

Thoroughly mix the ground spices and the rose petals. Larger quantities can also be mixed and stored in an airtight container.

PICKLES, PERSIAN (*TORSHIS*)

Whenever the *sofreh* or tablecloth is spread for a Persian meal, you will find a variety of pickles and relishes that, like chutneys in India, lend piquancy to the main courses. Most *torshis* are made from vegetables or fruits, spices, and good wine vinegar. Persian groceries usually stock a variety of them.

PISTACHIO (*PESTEH*)

These delicious nuts with their beautiful green color are native to Iran: Nicolaus of Damascus wrote in the first century BCE: "The youths of the Persians were taught to endure heat, cold, and rain; to cross torrents and to keep their armor and clothes dry; to pasture animals, to watch all night in the open air, and to subsist on wild fruit, such as pistachios, acorns, and wild pears." In Iran, pistachios are used for dishes ranging from

soup to desserts. The English term, among others, derives from the Persian.

Buy fresh pistachios unsalted in undyed shells. (Shells are sometimes dyed red to conceal imperfections.) After shelling, pistachios should be blanched to remove their papery skins: Drop the nuts into boiling water, boil about 1 minute, and drain. Lay a towel on a work surface, fold it over the nuts, and rub your hands lightly back and forth over the top, rolling the nuts to dislodge the skins. Spread the nuts on a baking sheet and dry them for 15 to 25 minutes in a 250°F oven.

PLUMS (*GOJEH*)

Fresh plums, in varieties ranging from purple to gold, are best bought during the summer months from local growers. In Iran, the small, round, green unripe variety known as *gojeh*—available in the U.S. in Persian groceries in the spring—are a favorite snack. They are also used as a souring agent in *khoresh*es and *ash*es and as a compote. For use throughout the year, different varieties of dried plums are sold at health food stores and Iranian groceries. They require only rinsing before use in a recipe.

POMEGRANATE (*ANAR*)

The red pomegranate, native to Iran and cultivated there for at least 4,000 years, is considered the fruit of heaven; in fact, it was probably the real "apple" in the Garden of Eden. The ancients commended it. Among them were King Solomon, who had a pomegranate orchard. And the Prophet Mohammad said, "Eat the pomegranate, for it purges the system of envy and hatred."

The fruit grows on large bushes or small trees, whose masses of crimson flowers brighten the pale mud walls of villages in Iran, Spain, and Italy. In Persian folk medicine, every part of the plant is believed to have virtue. The dried and powdered skin of the roots and fruit make a tea drunk to sweeten the breath, correct menstrual irregularity, kill parasites, and relieve nausea. Another tea, made from young shoots and leaves, fresh or dried, is a good remedy for nausea, lack of appetite, anemia, and headaches. The flowers repel insect pests—even honeybees avoid them—and provide yet a third tea, good for soothing uneasy stomachs.

Pomegranates, ranging in taste from sweet to

sour-sweet, have a special place in Iranian cookery. The fresh seeds (the edible part of the fruit), sprinkled with angelica powder, make a tart appetizer, and they add a bright note to green salads. Puréed and strained, the seeds produce a refreshing juice for drinking or for flavoring soups and stews. Or the juice may be reduced to a paste, a favorite souring agent, particularly in central and southern Iran. Most recipes that include pomegranate, which is classified as a cold food, also include hot foods like walnuts or ginger for balance.

Pomegranates are available in supermarkets in the fall and winter. Choose deep red fruits without blemishes. They will keep at home for about a week at room temperature. I have been able to keep them fresh at the end of the season for three weeks or more by wrapping them in newspaper and keeping them in the refrigerator drawer.

To seed a pomegranate, slice off the crown with a sharp knife. Make a superficial spiral cut in the skin around the pomegranate. Press both thumbs into the open crown and pull the fruit apart. Hold each segment seed-side-down over a bowl and tap the skin with a heavy spatula to dislodge the seeds from the membrane that holds them.

POMEGRANATE JUICE (AB-E ANAR)

In Iran fresh pomegranate juice is a popular drink, like orange juice, and is sold by juice vendors on street corners. In the West this juice is sold in health food stores and Persian groceries. Or you can make your own, allowing 2 large pomegranates for 1 cup of juice: Seed the pomegranates (see above), purée the seeds in a food processor, and strain the puree through a fine sieve. The juice will vary in sourness depending on the fruit; add sugar or lime juice to balance the taste to your liking.

POMEGRANATE, JUICED IN ITS SKIN (ABLAMBU)

This is a favorite amongst Iranians and it allows one to drink the juice of a pomegranate without fuss or mess. Choose a good-looking pomegranate with no blemishes or holes in the skin. Then, holding it in both hands with one thumb over the other, start by gently squeezing one of the raised parts of the fruit (there are usually four or five hills and valleys). The idea is to squeeze the seeds inside the skin without bursting the skin.

This needs to be done gently and systematically, going around the pomegranate until the whole fruit is soft and squishy. Then press it to your mouth and make a small hole in the skin with your teeth while you suck with your mouth and squeeze gently with your hands. You will get a very refreshing burst of juice in your mouth that is both delicious and sensual. Continue working around the fruit, squeezing and sucking, until you have drunk all the juice. It is an art that you will perfect with practice and once you know how you will never again see a good-looking pomegranate without wanting to *ablambu* it.

POMEGRANATE PASTE (ROB-E ANAR)

Pomegranate paste is available in specialty stores and Persian groceries both as a very sweet Persian brand and a very sour Arab brand. For Persian recipes, buy both types and mix them to achieve the proper sweet and sour taste. Or make your own paste. The following recipe requires 20 minutes' preparation and 1 hour's cooking, and yields about ½ pint:

Bring 8 cups fresh pomegranate juice (if the juice tastes sweet rather than sour, add the juice of 2 limes) to a boil in a non-reactive pot set over high heat.

Reduce the heat to medium, add 1 tablespoon salt, and simmer uncovered for 1 hour or more, stirring occasionally as the juice reduces. As it thickens to a paste, stir more frequently, to prevent sticking and burning.

Let the paste cool. Then store it in a clean, tightly closed jar in the refrigerator, where it will keep for a month, or in the freezer, where it will keep for a year. Or put the paste in a sterilized canning jar, process it in a boiling water canner for a few minutes, and store it in a cupboard.

QUINCE (BEH)

This big tree, a relative of the rose, is native to Iran, and cultivation probably started there, where the fruit's hard, astringent flesh, somewhere between an apple and a pear but with a special aromatic perfume, lends tartness to stews, jams, custards, and sherbet drinks. Its blossoms are also used to make a popular jam. Although quinces are available in supermarkets during the late autumn and winter, the biggest and best ones are sold in Persian groceries.

When shopping, choose firm, unblemished fruit. At the end of the season you can wrap individual quinces in newspaper and store them in the refrigerator drawer for 2 to 3 weeks.

Some varieties of Persian quinces can be eaten raw. The U.S. quince generally cannot. To prepare it for cooking, simply rub off the fuzz.

RHUBARB SYRUP

This recipe makes 1 pint of syrup and requires 10 minutes' preparation and 20 to 30 minutes' cooking:

2 pounds rhubarb, trimmed and rinsed
4 cups sugar
2 cups water
2 tablespoons lime juice

1. Bundle the rhubarb into a piece of doubled cheesecloth or muslin, and tie the ends securely with string to make a bag.
2. Bring the sugar and water to a boil over high heat. Reduce the heat to medium, drop in the bag of rhubarb, and simmer for 20 to 30 minutes. Remove the pan from the heat and let the contents cool.
3. Squeeze the cheesecloth bag over the cooled sugar water to extract every bit of rhubarb flavor. Discard the bag and the rhubarb.
4. Store the mixture in a jar in the refrigerator, where it will keep for several months.

RICE FLOUR (ARD-E BERENJ)

This delicate flour made from rice grains contains no gluten, so it cannot be used in bread making, but it is a fine thickener for *ashes*, *khoreshes*, puddings, and sweets, such as delicate rice cookies, a favorite in Iran. The flour is sold in supermarkets.

RICE STARCH (NESHASTEH-YE BERENJ)

This is a fine powder thickener, much like cornstarch, which may be substituted for it.

ROSE PETALS (GOL-E SORKH)

The blossoms of scented roses have lent flavor and color to food and drink since ancient times. In Persia there was a rose-petal wine; there is also rose-petal jam and rose-flavored honey; and rose petals flavor many sweet and savory dishes. Any scented rose petals may be used in cookery, provided they are free of pesticides, but dried ones are intense in flavor and convenient to use. They are sold in Persian groceries and health food stores.

ROSE WATER (GOLAB)

Few scents are more characteristic of Iran than that of rose water: It freshens the air in mosques and other public places; it is a part of every woman's makeup; and men use it as a cleanser for their moustaches and beards. Along with rose petals, it is a frequent ingredient in savory dishes and especially in pastries.

In Iran, rose water still is produced by ancient methods, primarily at Qamsar and Naisar, two small towns near Kashan, in the center of the country. Workers pick the roses in the early morning, when the scent is at its peak. The flowers are sent to a rose-water factory, where they are spread over the floor of a cool room and sorted. Then the fresh petals are steamed in a clay-sealed cauldron; the perfumed vapor rises through a bamboo pipe into a second pot set in cold running water. Cooling condenses the vapors into liquid rose water and the more intense oil of rose water. The first is bottled for cooking; the second is used for perfume; and the leftover rose petals are fed to animals.

Rose water is sold at Persian groceries. If it is kept cool, its aroma lasts for years.

SAFFRON (ZA'FERAN)

Saffron, believed to have originated in Iran, has been cultivated since prehistoric times: It was known to King Solomon and to the classical world. Today the saffron crocus, whose three stigmas form the spice, is cultivated not only in Iran, but throughout the Mediterranean, in India, and in China. It is the most expensive of spices, a fact that is easy to understand when you consider the amount of hand labor involved in harvesting the stigmas: It takes as many as 250,000 flowers to produce a pound of saffron. In Iran it is used as a dye, a medicine—it is believed to be an aphrodisiac and was sometimes sprinkled in newlyweds' beds—and for flavoring and coloring many dishes. Treated properly, saffron acts as a catalyst to give dishes a wonderful aroma and a beautiful bright orange color, distinctly different from turmeric.

When buying saffron, choose threads rather than powder, which is too often adulterated with turmeric. Threads should be ground with a cube of sugar, which helps the grinding process, then dissolved in hot water. The saffron-water solution can then be stored and used as needed. Never use the unground threads.

SUMAC (SOMAQ)

The red-berried sumac bush—*Rhus coriaria*, not to be confused with the poisonous white-berried species—provides one of the favorite flavorings for Persian cooking. To make it, the berries, along with leaves and branches, are boiled in water, then sieved to make sumac juice; or the berries alone are dried and crushed to a powder. The latter, sold in Persian groceries, is the more usual form of the spice; it is kept in the kitchen and on the table, along with salt and pepper.

Sumac is prized as a digestive, and even more prized as a pleasantly astringent souring agent: Iranians prefer its taste to that of lemon. It adds distinction to breads, marinades, soups, and stews, among other dishes. It is also delicious when sprinkled on kababs or onion salads or mixed with yogurt.

TAMARIND (TAMR-E HENDI)

A native of tropical East Africa or perhaps India (which is where the Persian name comes from), now widely grown, the tamarind tree bears pods that are used to make a souring agent indispensable not only in curries but in many Southern Iranian dishes. The partly dried, seeded pods are sold in Indian and Persian groceries, as are the liquid flavoring and the paste made from them. To make your own liquid or paste, see below.

TAMARIND LIQUID (AB-E TAMR-E HENDI)

Recipe is the same as for paste (below), only add water to dilute to desired consistency.

TAMARIND PASTE (ROB-E TAMR-E HENDI)

The following recipe, made from dried tamarind, requires 10 minutes' preparation, 40 minutes' cooking, and produces about ½ pint of liquid:

Place 1 pound dried tamarind pods in a large saucepan, cover them with 8 cups water, and bring them to a boil. Reduce the heat to medium and simmer uncovered for 30 minutes, adding more water if the pan becomes dry.

Place a fine mesh colander or strainer over a bowl and pour in the softened tamarind pods with their liquid. With a masher crush the pods to force out as much liquid as possible; you may pour a little boiling water over the pods to force more liquid out. Transfer the liquid to a clean, dry jar, cap tightly, and store in a cool, dark place or in the refrigerator.

TOMATOES (GOJEHFARANGI)

There is little to equal the taste of fresh ripe tomatoes in season; out of season, peeled, canned tomatoes make a good substitute. Most recipes require that fresh tomatoes be peeled. To do so, mark an X on the bottom of each tomato with a sharp knife. Plunge tomatoes into boiling water and blanch for 20 seconds, removing with a slotted spoon. Drain, and slip off the skin.

TURMERIC (ZARDCHUBEH)

Turmeric, a native of southeast Asia that is now grown in tropical climates throughout the world, comes from the rhizomes of a plant in the ginger family. Although the dried rhizomes are available, they are hard and difficult to grind. Ground turmeric is perfectly good.

WALNUTS (GERDU)

The walnut is native to Northern Iran and spread to the West and China from there. Walnuts feature in many Persian dishes, especially those containing pomegranates. Peeled and salted, they make a delicious snack. In Iran they are sold fresh in season by street vendors, who spend the day picking and peeling them. They store them in brine in glass jars and then sell them in the evening in bags of four, as roasted chestnuts are sold in winter.

To make a similar snack from dried walnuts, wash the nuts, place them in very hot water with 1 teaspoon of salt per pound of nuts, cover them, and refrigerate overnight. The next day, rub off the loosened skin and drop the nuts into a bowl of cold water until ready to use. Then drain the nuts and sprinkle them with salt to taste.

WHEY (*KASHK*)

In the West, whey means the thin liquid separated from milk curds during cheesemaking. In Iran, the term refers to drained, salted, sundried yogurt, used as a souring agent in many dishes. Whey is sold at Persian groceries. You may substitute sour cream.

YOGURT (*MAST*)

Health-giving yogurt is one of the oldest foods. The well-known tale of its invention goes like this: A desert nomad carried milk in his goatskin canteen. During his journey, heat and bacteria (lactobacillus) transformed the milk to yogurt. Taking a chance, the nomad drank it and was astonished to find it creamy and pleasantly sour. Having survived the experiment, he shared the discovery.

Whatever the real origin, yogurt is mentioned in records of ancient civilizations from India to Iran; by 500 BCE, holy men on the subcontinent had labeled the delicious mixture of yogurt and honey "the food of the gods." It reached western Europe in the sixteenth century. The first American yogurt company was established in 1931 in Massachusetts by the Armenian Colombosians family, whose Colombo yogurt is still on the market.

Almost every power has been ascribed to yogurt: It has variously been said to prolong life, increase sexual potency, remedy baldness, calm the nervous system, and cure skin diseases and gastrointestinal ailments. Whether it does these things or not, it forms a fine enrichment for many of the sauces, stews, and dips in this book. It is sold everywhere in low-fat and fat-free versions, or you can make your own (see YOGURT, HOMEMADE).

Any plain yogurt, store-bought or homemade, may be used in the recipes in this book: The choice depends on your taste and your diet. Creamy, homemade yogurt makes the richest, most unctuous sauces, but it is high in fat. Plain homemade yogurt is the next richest, followed by low-fat and fat-free commercial products.

YOGURT, DRAINED (*MAST-E KISEI*)

Many recipes call for drained, thick yogurt, which is simple to produce. If you are using commercial yogurt, pour the yogurt into a bowl and place the bowl in a larger one to catch drips.

Place three or four layers of paper towel on the surface of the yogurt, letting the edges overlap its bowl, and refrigerate for several hours. The towel will absorb excess moisture; discard it when the yogurt is thick.

If you are using homemade yogurt (see below), pour it into the center of a large square made of three layers of cheesecloth or muslin, draw the corners of the fabric together and tie them to make a bag—or use a cotton jelly bag—and hang the bag over a large pot. Let it hang for 15 to 20 minutes: The liquid, which may be discarded, will slowly drain from the yogurt, leaving it thick and creamy.

YOGURT, HOMEMADE (*MAST*)

When you prepare yogurt, make sure all your utensils are scrupulously clean: Dirty or greasy tools will not produce the desired result. This recipe requires 20 minutes' preparation and 12 hours' setting; it makes about 2 quarts of yogurt:

1. In a clean, non-reactive pot, bring 2 quarts whole milk to a boil over medium heat.

2. Immediately remove the milk from the heat and let it stand until cool but not completely cold. The temperature should be 115°F on a kitchen thermometer; the temperature is correct if you can just tolerate the heat on a finger for 20 seconds. (Temperature is important: If the milk is too cool, the culture will not grow; on the other hand, excess heat will kill the bacteria in the culture.)

3. Pour the milk into a square or rectangular glass dish. Pull out a rack in the center of the unheated oven and place the dish on it.

4. Place ¼ cup plain low-fat or fat-free commercial yogurt in each of the four corners of the dish. Gently push the rack back into the oven, and close the door. Do not turn on the oven but leave the light in the oven on to get just the right amount of warmth: The yogurt must rest undisturbed for at least 24 hours. An alternative is to cover and wrap the dish in a large towel or blanket and let it rest in a non-drafty corner of your kitchen.

5. When the yogurt is ready, store it in the refrigerator and use as needed.

Variation: To make creamy yogurt, add 1 cup half-and-half to the milk.

COOKING MEASUREMENTS

Note that all spoon and cup measurements used in this book are level. It is not easy to convert with absolute accuracy measurements for the kitchen, but absolute accuracy is usually not required (except for sauces, cakes and pastries). The tables below give the nearest convenient equivalents in both metric and British imperial measures while the formulas give a more precise conversion factor. British dry measures for ounces and pounds are the same as American measures. Liquid measures, however, are different.

LIQUID MEASURES

US	METRIC	UK (IMPERIAL)
1 teaspoon (⅓ tablespoon)	5 ml	1 teaspoon
2 teaspoons	10 ml	1 dessertspoon
1 tablespoon (3 teaspoons)	15 ml	1 tablespoon (½ fl. oz.)
2 tablespoons (⅛ cup)	30 ml	2 tablespoons
¼ cup (4 tablespoons)	60 ml	4 tablespoons
⅓ cup (5⅓ tablespoons)	80 ml	8 dessertspoons (2½ fl. oz.)
½ cup (8 tablespoons)	120 ml	scant ¼ pint (4 fl. oz.)
⅔ cup (10⅔ tablespoons)	160 ml	¼ pint
¾ cup (12 tablespoons)	180 ml	generous ¼ pint (6 fl. oz.)
1 cup (16 tablespoons)	240 ml	scant ½ pint (8 fl. oz.)
2 cups (1 pint, ½ quart or 16 fl. oz.)	480 ml	generous ¾ pint
2½ cups	600 ml	1 pint (20 fl. oz.)
3 cups (1½ pints or ¾ quart)	720 ml	1¼ pints
4 cups (2 pints or 1 quart)	960 ml	1½ pints (32 fl. oz.)
5 cups	1.2 liters	2 pints (1 quart, 40 fl. oz.)

LIQUID MEASURES

Cups x 0.24 = Liters
Liters x 4.23 = Cups

SOLID MEASURES

1 Pound = 16 Ounces
1 Kilo = 1000 Grams
Ounces x 28.35 = Grams
Grams x 0.035 = Ounces

OVEN TEMPERATURES

$°C = (°F − 32) ÷ 1.8$
$°F = (°C \times 1.8) + 32$

LINEAR MEASURES

US & UK	METRIC
¼ inch	6 mm
½ inch	13 mm
1 inch	2.5 cm
2 inches	5 cm
3 inches	7.5 cm
6 inches	15 cm
1 foot	30 cm

US & UK	METRIC
1 oz.	28 grams
3½ oz.	100 grams
¼ pound	112 grams
⅓ pound	150 grams
½ pound	225 grams
1 pound	450 grams
2.2 pounds	1 Kilogram

FAHRENHEIT	CENTIGRADE
200°	93°
250°	121°
300°	149°
350°	177°
400°	204°
450°	232°
500°	260°

𝒫ERSIAN GROCERIES & RESTAURANTS

This is a selected list of Persian speciality food stores and restaurants in or near major metropolitan areas. A more comprehensive list may be found on the publisher's web site at http://www.mage.com. If there is not a store near you, you may be able to get special ingredients via mail order. Kalustyan's (212-685-3451) in New York is one store that has a catalog and is equipped to take orders over the phone. Many other stores are not specifically set up for mail order, but will ship ingredients if you call and ask. More recently, there have been attempts to sell Persian goods over the Internet. One such site is http://bazaar.net, but others may have appeared since the publication of this book.

ATLANTA (GA)
Mirage Restaurant
6631 Roswell Rd.
Atlanta, GA 30328
(404) 843-8300

Omar Khayyam Restaurant
6435 Roswell Rd.
Atlanta, GA 30328
(404) 257-9090

Shahrzad International
215 Copeland Rd. #12
Atlanta, GA 30342
(404) 843-0549

BOSTON (MA)
Laleh Rokh Restaurant
97 Mt. Vernon St.
Boston, MA 02108
(617) 720-5511

Super Hero's Market
509 Mt. Auburn St.
Watertown, MA 02172
(617) 924-9507

Tabriz Bakery
56-A Mt. Auburn St.
Watertown, MA 02172
(617) 926-0880

CHICAGO (IL)
Arya Food Imports
5061 N. Clark St.
Chicago, IL 60640
(773) 878-2092

Pars Persian Store
5260 N. Clark St.
Chicago, IL 60640
(773) 769-6635

Reza Restaurant
5252 N. Clark St.
Chicago, IL 60640
(773) 561-1898

Reza Restaurant
432 W. Ontario
Chicago, IL 60610
(312) 664-4700

DALLAS (TX)
Andre Imported Foods
1478 W. Spring Valley
Richardson, TX 75080
(972) 644-7644

HOUSTON (TX)
Darband Kabob
5670 Hillcroft
Houston, TX 77036
(713) 975-8350

Garcons
2926 Hillcroft
Houston, TX 77057
(713) 781-0400

Super Vanak
5692 Hillcroft
Houston, TX 77036
(713) 952-7676

LAS VEGAS (NV)
Habib's Restaurant
4750 W. Sahara #24
Las Vegas, NV 89102
(702) 870-0860

Mediterranean Market
4147 S. Maryland Pkwy.
Las Vegas, NV 89119
(702) 731-6030

LOS ANGELES (CA)
Apadana Market & Deli
2865 E. Thousand Oaks
Thousand Oaks, CA 91360
(805) 496-0858

Bazjian Grocery
4725 Santa Monica Blvd.
Hollywood, CA 90029
(213) 663-1503

Caspian Restaurant
14100 Culver Dr.
Irvine, CA 92714
(714) 651-8454

Charlie Kabob
14 Santa Monica Pl.
Santa Monica, CA 90401
(310) 393-5535

Darband Restaurant
138 S. Beverly Dr.
Beverly Hills, CA 90212
(310) 859-8585

Downtown Kabab
934 S. Los Angeles St.
Los Angeles, CA 90015
(213) 612-0222

Pars Market
9016 W. Pico
Los Angeles, CA 90035
(310) 859-8125

Pouri Bakery
109 S. Adams Ave.
Glendale, CA 91205
(818) 244-4064

Sepah Market
14120 Culver Dr.
Irvine, CA 92714
(714) 552-8844

Shamshiri Restaurant
5229 Hollywood Blvd.
Hollywood, CA 90027
(213) 469-8434

Shiraz Restaurant
15472 Ventura Blvd.
Sherman Oaks, CA 91403
(818) 789-7788

Tehran Market
1417 Wilshire Blvd.
Santa Monica, CA 90403
(310) 393-6719

MIAMI (FL)
Shiraz Food Market
7397 SW 40th St.
Miami, FL 33155
(305) 264-8282

MILWAUKEE (WI)
Eastern Bazaar
3475 N. Oakland Ave.
Milwaukee, WI 53211
(414) 962-8998

MINNEAPOLIS (MN)
Caspian Bistro
2418 University Ave. SE
Minneapolis, MN 55414
(612) 623-1113

MONTREAL (PQ)
Akhavan Market
5768 Sherbrooke W.
Montreal, PQ H4A 1X1
(514) 485-4887

Main Importing Grocery
1188 St. Laurant
Montreal, PQ H2X 2S5
(514) 861-5681

NASHVILLE (TN)
International Food Market
206 Thompson Ln.
Nashville, TN 37211
(615) 333-9651

NEW YORK (NY)
Caravan Restaurant
741 Eighth Ave.
New York, NY 10036
(212) 262-2021

Kababi-e-Nader
48 East 29th Ave.
New York, NY 10016
(212) 683-4833

Kalustyan's
123 Lexington Ave.
New York, NY 10016
(212) 685-3451

Nader International Food
1 East 28th St.
Flushing, NY 10016
(212) 686-5793

Panahi Iransuper
1729 Second Ave.
New York, NY 10128
(212) 348-5050

Pars International Produce
145 West 30th St.
New York, NY 10021
(212) 760-7277

Persepolis Restaurant
1423 Second Ave.
New York, NY 10021
(212) 535-1100

OKLAHOMA CITY (OK)
Travel by Taste
Market & Restaurant
4818 N. McArthur
Warr Acres, OK 73122
(405) 787-2969

OTTAWA (ON)
Ayoub's Market
322 Sommerset St. E
Ottawa, ON A1L 6W3
(613) 233-6417

PHILADELPHIA (PA)
Persian Grille
637 Germantown Rd.
Lafayette Hill, PA 19444
(215) 825-2705

PHOENIX (AZ)
Apadana Restaurant
2924 N. Scottsdale Rd.
Tempe, AZ 85281
(602) 945-5900

Haji Baba
Market & Restaurant
1513 E. Apache
Tempe, AZ 85281
(602) 894-1905

PORTLAND (OR)
International Food Bazaar
915 SW Ninth Ave.
Portland, OR 97205
(503) 228-1960

Kolbeh Restaurant
& Mediterranean Market
11830 SW Kerr Pkwy.
Lake Oswego, OR 97035
(503) 246-8227

RALEIGH (NC)
Caspian Int'l Market
2909 Brentwood Rd.
Raleigh, NC 27604
(919) 954-0029

SAN DIEGO (CA)
Aria International Market
2710 Garnet Ave. #205
San Diego, CA 92109
(781) 274-9632

Bandar Restaurant
825 4th Ave.
San Diego, CA 92101
(614) 238-0101

SAN FRANCISCO (CA)
Attari Deli
156 W. El Camino Real
Sunnyvale, CA 94087
(408) 773-0290

Chelokababi
1236 Wolford El Camino
Sunnyvale, CA 94086
(408) 737-1222

Farm Fresh Persian Grocery
10021 S. Blaney Ave.
Cupertino, CA 95608
(408) 257-3746

Faz Restaurant
161 Sutter St.
San Francisco, CA 94104
(415) 362-0404

Faz Restaurant
5121 Hopyard Rd.
Pleasanton, CA 94588
(925) 460-0444

Faz Restaurant
600 Hartz Ave.
Danville, CA 94526
(510) 838-1320

Royal Food Market
1602 Washington Blvd.
Fremont, CA 94539
(510) 668-1107

United Food Market
1965 Foxworthy Ave.
San Jose, CA 95124
(408) 559-6444

SEATTLE (WA)
Caspian Restaurant & Grill
5517 University Way NE
Seattle, WA 98105
(206) 524-3434

Kolbeh Restaurant
1956 First Ave. S
Seattle, WA 98134
(206) 224-9999

Pars Market
13422 NE 20th St.
Bellevue, WA 98005
(425) 641-5265

Rooz Supermarket
12332 Lake City Way NE
Seattle, WA 98125
(206) 363-8639

TORONTO (ON)
Asy Max
5545 Yonge St.
Willowdale, ON M2N 5S3
(416) 250-6100

Darvish Restaurant
6087 Yonge St.
N. York, ON M2M 3W2
(416) 226-9028

Lavash Bread Bakery
3862 Chesswood Dr.
N. York, ON M3G 2W6
(416) 398-9121

VANCOUVER (BC)
Bijan Specialty Food
1461 Clyde Ave.
W. Vancouver, BC V7T 1E9
(604) 925-1055

Caspian Restaurant
1495 Marion Dr.
W. Vancouver, BC
(604) 921-1311

Pars Deli Market
1801 Lonsdale Ave.
N. Vancouver, BC V7M 2J8
(604) 988-3515

Persepolis Restaurant
112 E 13th St.
N. Vancouver, BC
(604) 990-0001

Yas Bakery
1528 Lonsdale Ave.
N. Vancouver, BC V7M 2J4
(604) 990-9006

WASHINGTON, D.C.
Assal Market I
118 West Maple Ave.
Vienna, VA 22180
(703) 281-2248

Assal Market II
6039 Leesburg Pike
Falls Church, VA 22041
(703) 578-3232

International Market & Deli
2010 P St. NW
Washington, DC 20009
(202) 293-0499

Moby Dick House of Kabab
1070 31st St. NW
Washington, DC 20007
(202) 333-4400

Neam's Market
3217 P St. NW
Washington, DC 20007
(202) 338-4694

Paradise Restaurant
7141 Wisconsin Ave.
Bethesda, MD 20814
(301) 907-7500

Yas Bakery
114 E. Fairfax St.
Falls Church, VA 22046
(703) 237-9271

Yas Bakery
7855 Rockville Pike
Rockville, MD 20852
(301) 762-5416

Yekta Grocery
1488 Rockville Pike
Rockville, MD 20852
(301) 984-1190

INDEX